Environmental Law, Ethics & Governance

Environmental Law, Ethics & Governance

Edited by

Erika Techera

Inter-Disciplinary Press

Oxford, United Kingdom

© Inter-Disciplinary Press 2010
http://www.inter-disciplinary.net/publishing/id-press/

The *Inter-Disciplinary Press* is part of *Inter-Disciplinary.Net* – a global network for research and publishing. The *Inter-Disciplinary Press* aims to promote and encourage the kind of work which is collaborative, innovative, imaginative, and which provides an exemplar for inter-disciplinary and multi-disciplinary publishing.

Inter-Disciplinary Press, Priory House, 149B Wroslyn Road, Freeland, Oxfordshire. OX29 8HR, United Kingdom.
+44 (0)1993 882087

British Library Cataloguing in Publication Data. A catalogue record for this book is available from the British Library.

ISBN: 978-1-84888-034-4
First published in the United Kingdom in paperback in 2010. First edition.

Cover design by Peter Day.

Table of Contents

Preface

Erika Techera

The idea for this volume emerged on the final day of the *8th Global Conference on Environmental Justice and Global Citizenship* held at Mansfield College, Oxford from 10th to 12th July 2009. The main topics of that conference were environmental ethics, sustainability and education. The participants included representatives from many parts of the globe including the Philippines and Indonesia, Uganda and South Africa, Australia and New Zealand, the United Kingdom, Denmark and Malta, the United States of America and Canada. Equally diverse were the discipline areas from which the presenters came: law, philosophy, ethics, physical and social sciences. Several key themes emerged from the presentation of papers, the discussion that followed and the intellectual debate over the three days. This volume comprises seven chapters linked to one strand of that conversation - the role of law and ethics in achieving good environmental governance.

Environmental Law, Ethics and Governance aims to inspire further research regarding the ethical dimensions of environmental law and legal governance. It draws attention to the important role that law can play but also the necessity for inter-disciplinarity in our approaches to regulatory, educational and philosophical future challenges. The individual chapters deal with a number of issues concerning the role of law in altering our environmental ethic; and also how environmental ethics can be embedded in law and legal thinking in order to bring about a change in human behaviour. Given the overarching goal of improving environmental governance, the chapters also address the important issue of how law and legal regulation can become more interconnected with and embrace ideas from other discipline areas.

The book provides a valuable and timely contribution to the discourse in this area. Despite an expansion of international treaties, national legislation and local initiatives over the last thirty-five years, many environmental problems persist and in some cases degradation has worsened. Achieving good environmental governance remains a significant challenge. Therefore new approaches must be sought which facilitate positive environmental outcomes and the development of more effective legal regimes and governance options. This is particularly pressing in the face of such critical contemporary concerns such as climate change.

This volume is a stimulating and informative publication covering the academic research and professional experiences of a diversity of authors engaged in the achievement of environmental justice and good environmental governance. The book is divided into three sections. The task of dividing up the papers was not an easy one because as the reader will see there are

considerable linkages between the different chapters. One of the strengths of
this book is the diversity of topics covered, each of which is interconnected
by reflections upon ethical considerations. Another common thread is that of
good environmental governance, be it of a physical area, an environmental
problem or a natural resource. Governance issues arise at all levels from the
global to the local and the case studies explored in this book provide
excellent examples from across this range. Lastly, it will be seen that the
chapters address process and procedure as well as substantive issues. The
authors consider, for example, how new law ought to be drafted, the
implementation of that law and environmental legal education. It is clear that
these topics remain of great significance if law and policy is to be effective

The book commences with a section entitled *Contemporary Issues
in Environmental Law*. This sets the tone and provides the backdrop for the
entire volume. It includes three chapters, the first of which is by Harriet
Nakulenge entitled *Environmental Ethics is the Key to Sustainability in
Contemporary Society*. Harriet is a practising state attorney in the Republic of
Uganda and in her chapter she provides a concise introduction to
environmental philosophy and ethics. She reflects upon how our
philosophical beliefs about nature shape the law, but also how law can
influence our environmental ethic. These two roles of law are a common
theme recurring throughout the book. Harriet draws attention to the
difficulties of drafting laws and policies which facilitate a change in human
behaviour at individual, national and global levels - to create a moral duty to
protect nature and natural resources.

The second chapter is written by Brad Jessup, a Teaching Fellow at
the Australian National University College of Law in Australia. His chapter
is entitled *Investing the Law with an Environmental Ethic: Using an
Environmental Justice Theory for Change*. Brad contends that the acceptance
of sustainability as the dominant paradigm in environmental governance has
not had the effect of creating a new ethic. He argues for the introduction of a
broad theory of environmental justice into law and calls for a domestic
environmental legal system which limits the unfair distribution of
environmental harm and incorporates the principles of sustainable
development. He draws attention to key areas of environmental law where
such reform might best be achieved including standing provisions and
funding of litigation, environmental assessment, biodiversity conservation
and pollution regulation.

The third chapter in this section, *Teaching Environmental Law in
the 21st Century,* is written by myself and addresses environmental legal
education. With the evolution of environmental laws, both globally and
domestically, teaching in this area has become much more complex.
However, the increasing interconnectedness of legal issues with other areas
of environmental studies necessitates a reconsideration of the way in which

this subject is taught. I draw upon my own experience teaching environmental law, to undergraduate and postgraduate students, and reflect upon whether curricula and methodologies must now be adjusted to better equip graduates with the multi- and inter-disciplinary skills needed in the practice and application of environmental law and principles.

The second part of this volume is entitled *International Environmental Governance*. This section revisits some existing legal governance regimes and concepts but with a focus upon present and future challenges. There are two chapters in this section. The first is written by Jane Verbitsky, who is a senior lecturer at Auckland University of Technology in New Zealand. Her contribution is entitled *Antarctica: The Ticking Clock* in which she explores the triumph of the Antarctic Treaty System in successfully governing this region of the world for over fifty years. However, she queries whether this regime is equipped to face contemporary environmental governance issues such as tourism. In particular she addresses the question of whether this unique area of the world would be better protected if it were declared to be a common heritage territory, world park or natural reserve. She draws attention to the importance of these issues at this time and the necessity of identifying a robust governance mechanism to secure Antarctica's future.

The next chapter is written by Bridget Lewis, an associate lecturer at the Queensland University of Technology in Australia. In *The Role of Human Rights in Environmental Governance: The Challenge of Climate Change* she considers emerging environmental rights and in particular the right to a healthy environment. She explores the benefits of a human rights framework and advocates greater consideration of human rights norms in the development of legal strategies to overcome contemporary environmental problems such as climate change. She refers to the Torres Strait Islands and the challenges the indigenous people face, to illustrate the impacts of climate change. The chapter connects with several of the underlying themes that run throughout this volume, particularly in terms of applying human rights approaches in addressing injustice in the context of the current climate change crisis.

The final section of the book, *Perspectives on domestic regulation*, includes two very different case studies. One relates to land use in Australia and the other to the construction industry in the United Kingdom. Nevertheless they are both linked by underlying concepts of property. Jo Kehoe is a lecturer in law at the Central Queensland University in Australia. Her chapter, *Rural Landholders in Queensland Australia and the Politics of Environmental Law*, considers the political phases, systems and ideologies which have shaped responses to a significant natural resource issue in Australia - native vegetation management. She provides us with a critique of a controversial piece of legislation the *Vegetation Management Act 1999* and goes on to argue that the process by which it was made fetters the progression of environmental justice in that state. She concludes that the environment is not beyond political expediency and therefore it remains necessary to constantly analyse political processes and systems to ensure they are truly representative and meet the needs of society.

The final chapter is written by Francine Baker, a practising solicitor. In *Climate Change Construction and Environmental Accountability* she explores the recently enacted UK *Climate Change Act 2008* from the perspective of the property and construction industry and the achievement of environmental justice. She analyses specific features of this legislation including the independent committee established to assess and address climate change issues. In linking her chapter to the central themes of this volume Francine argues that the enactment of this legislation does not of itself mean that a new environmental ethic has been adopted and she calls for further developments to ensure that the Act achieves this outcome.

The above analysis demonstrates that *Environmental Law, Ethics and Governance* includes a selection of papers that are at once broad in their coverage of thematic issues and at times sharply focused on specific environmental concerns. Collectively, they draw attention to the importance of cross-disciplinary research in a number of interconnected areas: environmental justice and overcoming injustice; legislation, law-making and legal education; strategies and approaches to achieving good governance; and environmental ethics, philosophy and shaping human attitudes towards nature. No doubt this book will be of considerable interest to law- and policy-makers, practitioners, researchers and all those who are involved in the achievement of good environmental governance.

I am very pleased to have been involved in the conference and also the preparation of such a powerful collection. This volume makes an insightful contribution to the literature in this area. I would like to thank Inter-Disciplinary.Net for again providing a fabulous opportunity for inter- and multi-disciplinary discourse in the important areas of environmental justice and global citizenship. Special thanks go to Ram Vemuri for leading the conference and Nancy Billias and Daniel Riha for the production of this volume. For my own part I am very grateful for the assistance of two excellent student editors who helped in the preparation of this book.

Erika Techera
Centre for International & Environmental Law
Macquarie Law School
Macquarie University
Sydney, Australia

PART I

Contemporary Issues in Environmental Law

Environmental Ethics is the Key to Sustainability in Contemporary Society

Harriet Nalukenge

Abstract

Environmental ethics is the discipline that studies the moral relationship of human beings to, and also the value and moral status of, the environment and its non-human content. The way people interact with the environment depends on the ethics of a particular individual or society. The outcome of such interaction affects both the quantity and quality of environmental resources. Studies show that the instrumental and intrinsic value of items in the environment generates a moral duty to protect them. Many perspectives assign a greater amount of intrinsic value to human beings than to non-human things. This chapter demonstrates the difficulties of formulating policies and best practice that could change these attitudes. The views of emerging thinkers indicate that social and political order has an ethical basis. Ideas are advanced to show that the ecological context shapes human organisation and behaviour and the human context in turn shapes ecological organisation and response. Further, the chapter raises arguments to show that it is not property rights regimes that matter but rather the rules governing use.

Key Words: Ecosystem, environmental ethics, morality, ecology, legal philosophy.

*****

1.   Introduction

Environmental ethics concerns itself with formulating our moral obligations regarding the environment. This enterprise is meant to engage with the real world. Ethics seeks a critical grasp of the principles and standards that guide a person in making morally right choices in his or her daily activities. It involves intelligent judgement and voluntary action wherever a problem of right and wrong conduct confronts us; humans face a choice between alternative values. Moral judgement must be conceived within the person, himself or herself, with the principle on which he or she proposes to act. An action is morally good only if the principle which is manifested in it is right.

The common interest of all states is the need to ensure wise and equitable use of living and non-living resources, which requires avoidance of over-exploitation. The effectiveness of states and governments in achieving this outcome will affect the types of ethics that emerge. In turn ethics must propose alternative and better means of resolving the environmental problems people face. Ethical behaviour can inspire a collaborative culture of new thinking and the development of unconventional ideas that push for change in an unexpected way. This chapter considers both how ethics shapes our responses to environmental issues and also demonstrates the difficulties of crafting schemes that promote better stewardship and resilience for the conservation of natural resources.

A. The State of the Environment Today

The environment is the totality of human surroundings, natural or constructed, spatial, social and temporal. It is an extension of ourselves, its well-being requiring the same care as our own health.[1] It comprises three major parts; the physical component which consists of the atmosphere (the layer of the air that surrounds the Earth), the hydrosphere (the waters on the Earth's surface and underground) and the lithosphere (the solid and weathered rocks that make up the earth). The second component is biological, consisting of all living things; while the socio-cultural includes culture, traditions, education, religion human activities and relationships. All three components are inter-dependent and from an anthropocentric perspective human beings are at the centre.

Human activities are transforming the environment and there are many causes for these changes including population increase, urbanisation and industrialisation. Environmental policies in many countries recognise this and underscore the need to re-orient national and local efforts to address environmental problems in a more comprehensive and integrated manner.

B. Justification for the Sustainable Utilisation of Nature

There are several reasons to support the preservation of endangered species. An aesthetic justification contends that biodiversity contributes to the quality of life because nature is appreciated for its unique physical beauty. The aesthetic role of nature in all its diverse forms is reflected in the art and literature of every culture, attaining symbolic status in the spiritual life of many different communities. Groups in the medical and pharmacological fields support another justification. It is argued that nature has an ecological advantage, meaning that every species provides important functions that are beneficial to the survival of humans. Therefore, people need to preserve the natural environment in order to retain a balance in nature that is ultimately beneficial to humankind. There is also a moral justification for the preservation of nature. The moralists argue that all species have a right to exist and as such it is incumbent upon the human species to protect them and ensure their continued existence. There is therefore an urgent call for humans to identify measures to preserve nature. These measures include environmental education and advocacy.

2.   Sustainability
A. The Ethical Approach to Sustainability

Sustainability is a human construct in that humans use their environment for a range of objectives, including subsistence, commodity production, aesthetic pleasure and indirect ecosystem services. These objectives have their basis in the desire to sustain human life, enhance standards of living, maintain culture and protect environmental quality for generations to follow. The different objectives for the use of environmental resources lead to different expectations as to what is to be sustained and who is to have claims on environmental services.

Equity is an important aspect of a just approach to sustainability. From an environmental viewpoint sustainable development focuses on the stability of biological and physical systems. The emphasis is on preserving the resilience and dynamic ability of such systems to adapt to change, rather than conservation of some ideal 'static' condition. It is recognised that natural resource degradation, pollution and loss of biodiversity reduce this system resilience.

Reconciling these various issues and implementing approaches to them as a means to achieve sustainable development is a formidable task, since all three elements of sustainable development must be given balanced consideration. Protection of the environment is a major objective of sustainable development. Best practice economic development, for example, ultimately depends on the institutions that can protect and maintain the environment's carrying capacity and resilience.[2] The ethics and behaviour of humans in relation to their use of the environment is critical to the design and implementation of effective environmental protection.

It should be noted that ethics and rules can be effective in modulating the interaction between humans and their environment but they must reflect both general principles and specific social and ecological contexts. Ecological contexts contain the structure of ecosystems in which humans live and work, as well as the particular functional properties of those ecosystems. The particular details of the social and ecological context are what give human environmental interaction its variety of detail.

B. Morality and Sustainability

A minimal conception of morality limits itself to those rules which are a condition of the existence of society; whereas a more comprehensive conception of morality would embrace the entire body of rules governing a community or class. The individual in turn is conditioned to accept the socio-legal norms as controlling his or her entire life and precluding the formation of individual values. It must be pointed out here that ethics unlike law helps to build individual values. Therefore international environmental laws should reflect the current social morality which advances ethical conduct.

C. Environmental Attitudes in Relation to Sustainability

Environmental attitudes are tendencies to respond favourably or unfavourably towards one's surroundings. The focus of this chapter is that an ethic is more effective at changing attitudes and behaviour, both of which are important in promoting sustainability in contemporary society. Just as with many other attitudes, environmental attitudes can be measured in terms of the individual's emotional reactions; for example, negative feelings towards vandalism or rubbish, beliefs such as littering is bad and behavioural attitudes such as avoiding bad environmental practices or taking positive care of the environment.

According to Barron and Graziano research on environmental attitudes has focused on issues such as the extent of public awareness about environmental problems and the degree of consistency among people's beliefs and behaviour relative to the improvement of environmental conditions.[3] Attitudes are assumed to be relatively enduring. This means that once established people's evaluation of issues is usually stable over time. Also because attitudes are comparatively long-lasting they need to be studied, measured and then may be used to predict action. The other point to note is that attitudes are learnt. People are not born with attitudes, for instance towards environmental pollution, they develop them, good or bad, through experience and exposure.

Barron and Graziano further reiterate that psychologists have studied the process of attitude formulation and this has made it possible to develop programs that may encourage desirable attitudes. For example increasing favourability towards energy conservation.[4]

Attitudes influence how people process information about the world. They also influence behaviour. That is to say people's actions reflect evaluations of relevant issues. Allport defined attitudes as a predisposition to respond in a consistent manner toward objects and situations to which the attitude is related.[5] They recommend that researchers should therefore continue to focus on behavioural implications of attitudes. Thus if people are to understand, predict and influence human behaviour, they must investigate and understand attitudes.

Research in this area is crucial. Authors such as Palmer and Neal[6] believe that promoting positive attitudes to the environment is essential.

D. Human Participation and Practices that Affect the Environment

Human attitudes do not harm or help the environment. Human behaviour (practices) on the other hand, can cause significant harm, yet hold a great deal of hope for helping the environment. Therefore, people who work towards environmental sustainability must address human practices and behaviour.

Day and Monroe wrote that human practices are key elements that both contribute to and help resolve environmental problems.[7] Furthermore, Lefton reports that many day-to-day practices are determined by a person's behaviour, and practices are usually determined by a person's attitudes and how strongly those attitudes are held.[8] He suggests that a person's attitudes, awareness, experiences and practices are inter-related.

According to Baron and Graziano,[9] practices are closely related to behaviour. Day and Monroe[10] state that behaviour is what people do, a single observable action performed by an individual, while practices are a series of related behaviours. People perform a host of environmentally appropriate and inappropriate behaviours every day, which make up their practices. Although behaviour may be performed by habit, it could also be the outcome of a conscious decision. They believe that practices are a series of related behaviours. For example, recycling waste is a practice which can be broken down into many separate observable behaviours; for example separating glass, cans, paper and organic material into different containers.

3.   Traditional Knowledge and Environmental Ethics
A. The Role of Traditional Knowledge in Promoting Environmental Ethics

Warren defines traditional knowledge as that knowledge which is unique to a given culture or society.[11] Traditional knowledge has been used by most African societies as a basis for decision making in agriculture, health care, food preparation, education, natural resources, management and other activities in rural communities. Traditional knowledge is embedded in community practices, institutions, relationships and rituals.

Tradition has a special strength because it is associated with emotional attachments to family, religion, race, language and folk history. Tradition appears to be spontaneous and timeless, the way of nature or the gods. 'That's just the way things are' and it has always been done that way are the essential ingredients of tradition. In many societies, government and law are rooted in religion and social custom.

One link between ecological and human systems is developed through local knowledge, also called traditional ecological knowledge or Indigenous knowledge. There are many forms of knowledge about both ecological and human systems which are not generated scientifically but rather result from years of direct work experience, customs and practices with respect to the environment. These customs and practices are often operational expressions of traditional knowledge about the structure and function of environmental resources. For example, villagers in India acquire and use traditional ecological knowledge in the course of their day-to-day work, which links them to the environment.[12]

Whether based on religion, race or custom, natural traditions and symbols arouse emotion and create feelings automatically without requiring thought or learning on the part of the populace. The traditions need not be rational, moral or practical, only generally accepted and in many cases old. Even the symbols that originally had a practical or moral purpose lose that function in the popular mind over a period of years.

In Africa, Indigenous traditions contain symbolic and ethical messages that are passed from generation to generation in order to ensure respect and compassion for other living creatures. These are in the form of taboos and myths. Many local organisations, institutions and communities have a wealth of information about Indigenous knowledge practices. However these practices are not disseminated effectively because community-based organisations lack the capacity to capture, document, validate and share them.

Many aspects of the environment and its conservation were found embedded in traditional African values and structures. According to James Kamara environmental resources are not just factors of production with economic significance but also have their place within the sanctity of nature.[13] In Africa certain places have spiritual significance and are used as locations for rituals and sacrifices; for example, sacred groves, caves, mountains, trees and rivers.

These locations are quite often patches of high biodiversity which are well-conserved and protected by the community. These features were kept natural until the adoption of modern practices and the abandonment of traditional values. Specific plants and animals were protected using traditional taboos and rituals. Activities such as hunting and collection of medicinal plants were all regulated by either confining them to a particular time of year, such as during festivals, or left to particular people to harvest.

It is important to note that not all indigenous knowledge is environmentally friendly. So caution should be exercised when advocating Indigenous knowledge as a means to stop environmental degradation. It can also be argued that some of these traditional beliefs and values are no longer relevant today because of economic changes, population pressure, civil wars, politics and other dynamics in society.

Despite the above arguments the positive role that traditions and Indigenous values could play in ensuring sustainable use of the environment cannot be underestimated. Principle 22 of the Rio Declaration highlights the important issue of recognising that the special knowledge of Indigenous people is an important aspect of environmental management and development. Governments and inter-governmental organisations should empower Indigenous people and their communities to protect the environment through the use of relevant traditional knowledge.

B. Challenges to the Promotion of Traditional Knowledge

A major challenge for the design of environmental ethics and rules is to ensure that decision makers have the appropriate incentives to take such equilibrium shifts into account and to make the appropriate tradeoffs between the social costs and benefits to society at large. This requires monitoring feedback from the ecological system when making decisions and allowing perturbations to enter the system at a scale that allows sub-systems variability but does not challenge the underlying ecological and economic activity.[14]

The need to understand the relationship between poverty, population and the environment is critical. Expanding populations which exacerbate economic, social and ecological impoverishment make all the existing environmental problems more critical.[15] It so happens that in places where traditions are practiced, poverty and demographic issues hinder sustainable use of the environment. In East Africa for example people produce many children due to the desperation induced by poverty. Ethical practices are important in changing people's attitudes towards the environment; however population growth and poverty have to be controlled otherwise ethics will be less effective.

4. Property Rights, Regimes and Law

In talking about ethics, property rights and laws must also be considered. Property rights regimes matter to the use of environmental resources, a fact that has been well established, if not always practised.

Garret Hardin's article the 'Tragedy of the Commons'[16] focused widespread attention on the problem of environmental degradation in the absence of rules governing use. He argued that collectively owned property was the culprit of degradation and that private property is necessary to sustain environmental practices.

This author however holds the opinion, which is also based on scientific evidence, that sustaining environmental resources is not dependant on a particular structure of property law but rather on a well-specified property rights regime and a congruency of that regime with the ecological and social context.

5. Philosophy and Environmental Ethics

A. Contribution of the Great Philosophers

Numerous philosophers have written on this topic although it only really developed in the 1970s following increased environmental awareness in the 1960s about the effects that technology, industrial economic expansion and population growth were having on the environment. Some moralists such as Hobbes have concentrated on people's native egoism and insatiate greed. They point out that self regard and benevolence are both natural to man.[17]

Aristotle, unlike Machiavelli, argued that social and political order has by right an ethical basis. It is not imposed on its subjects but itself grows out of the tissue of the institution of normal human life.[18]

Radical ecologists are of the view that ethical extensionalism is inadequate because it is stuck in traditional ways of thinking that led to those environmental problems in the first place. Their opinion is that it is too human-centred.[19] Whereas social ecologists and deep ecologists are of the view that environmental crisis lies in the dominant ideology of western societies.[20] Eco-feminists however point to the link between social domination and the control of the natural world.[21] By the mid 1970s feminists had raised the issue of whether patriarchal modes of thinking encouraged not only widespread demeaning and colonising of women but also people of colour, animals and nature. Eco-feminism calls for the radical overhaul of the prevailing philosophical perspective and ideology of western society.

B. Philosophical Reflection on the Concept of Justice

Hart argued that unless legal and moral justice are held firmly apart in the mind of the community, the only mode of denunciation of evil laws is to call them no law, an artificial and unconvincing usage.[22] Hart's legal philosophy advances the idea that ethics should be incorporated into legislation to promote the interests of the public. Humans are given greater intrinsic value. This gives them power to advance their selfish ends. Therefore, the moral duties people have towards the environment are derived from their direct duty to other inhabitants.

The instrumental and intrinsic value of items in the environment therefore generates moral duty on the part of moral agents to protect it or at least to refrain from damaging it.[23] Many ethical perspectives assign a significantly greater amount of intrinsic value to human beings than to any non-human things such that the protection or promotion of human interests or well-being, at the expense of non-human things, turns out to be nearly always justified. Such destruction might damage the well-being of humans now and in the future, since our welfare is essentially dependant on a sustainable environment.[24]

Environmental ethics poses a challenge to traditional anthropocentrism. In the first place, it questions the assumed moral superiority of human beings over members of other species on Earth. Secondly, it investigates the possibility of rational arguments for assigning intrinsic value to the natural environment and its non-human content.

6.   Ethics and Legal Theory

Ethics is the sphere of ideal forms of life determined by individuals for themselves. On the other hand morality denotes rules or principles governing human behaviour which apply universally within a community or class. As noted above, a 'minimal conception of morality' is limited to those rules which are a condition for existence, whereas a more complete conception would embrace all the rules governing a society. This approach illuminates the tripartite relation between:

a) the values that individuals, as conscientious and responsible human beings, set themselves;

b) the moral norms governing a society which reflects a social balance and choice between conflicting individual values; and

c) the legal order, which must reflect the current social morality but is far from identical to it.

The norms of social behaviour are set by a superior who exercises complete legislative authority, and whose law-making power is used to direct and control every aspect and element of social behaviour. The individual in turn is conditioned to accept the socio-legal norms as controlling his or her entire life and precluding the formation of individual values which would be 'ungodly'.[25]

In every contemporary society there is some tension between the three orders of conduct which are spheres of law, morality and ethics. In pluralistic and relatively individualistic society, which characterises the value system of modern democracy, the tension between these three spheres is and must be considerable. There is an increasingly active reciprocal inter-relationship between the legal and moral order. On the one hand moral values press upon the legal system, and on the other, the modern law-maker can, to an increasing extent, influence and modify the social habits of the community.

Kant in his critique of practical reason distinguishes law from morals by characterising law as being concerned with internal conduct;[26] many moral and legal philosophers have also adopted this distinction.[27] A legal system that makes punishment or civil obligation dependent upon malicious intention or capacity to control one's actions reaches into the inner mind of people. Modern psychology has refined and enlarged the inter-relationship between the inner workings of the mind and external conduct. Even more barren is the converse proposition that morality is only concerned with internal conduct. Morality helps to clarify the distinction between ethical individual value judgements and social conduct. Instead of watertight and artificial divisions of the three distinct spheres, there is a fluid inter-relationship, variable with regard to the separation and inter-penetration of the three spheres according to the character of the society in question.[28]

Ethical theories have a considerable influence on legal theory. Ethical theories regard certain basic principles of conduct as essential to a satisfactory legal order, not as a matter of *a priori* postulates set by God or reason (natural law) but as matter of social experience. For example, the social contract theories which are predicated on the assumption that humans need to restrain their appetites for violence, greed and domination in order to achieve a minimum of mutual protection and security.

Modernisation of the social contract philosophy in its five principles provides that:

a)   human vulnerability makes it necessary for a legal order to restrict the use of violence;

b)   approximate equality makes it necessary for a legal system to develop rules of mutual forbearance and compromise;

c)   limited altruism makes it necessary to have some provisions to restrain tendencies towards aggression;

d)   limited resources makes it necessary to provide some system of exchange or joint planning of services and goods;

e)   limited understanding and strength of will compels the need for a system of voluntary cooperation within a coercive regime.

Thus the maxims of conduct, which many of the older natural law philosophers have presented as flowing from the immutable nature of man, are here presented as having been shown by experience and history to be necessary for the survival of man in civilisation. The above advances the idea that ethics should be incorporated into all legislation to regulate behaviour.[29]

7.   **International Aspects**
A. Government and Inter-Governmental Organisations

Whenever humans gather together there is need for government; a mutually understood system that will allow decisions to be made effectively and facilitate a division of responsibilities to ensure the survival of the group. In this sense even the most isolated family develops the basic elements of a government and with that organisation comes a kind of law.

The world is in part governed by amalgamations of countries in inter-governmental organisations. Social, industrial and agricultural patterns seldom conform to national boundaries, so inter-governmental organisations are needed to address the concerns shared by nations. This need has increased in modern times because of the shrinking world created by 20th century improvements in communication and transportation.

Famous inter-governmental organisations like the United Nations are an important forum for international discussion. There is a continuing need for other inter-governmental organisations that are devoted to specialised needs or to specifically regional concerns.

The environment should be a major concern of inter-governmental agencies because its use affects nearly all peoples. Other inter-governmental organisations such as the Commonwealth fulfil the same need for collaboration on concerns that cross national boundaries.

B. State Responsibility in International Law

State responsibility or international liability is the principle by which states may be held accountable in interstate claims under international law. The foundation of responsibility in most cases lies in the breach of obligations undertaken by states or imposed upon them by international law. Responsibility in environmental cases will normally arise either because of one or more of the customary obligations or because of a breach of a treaty.

A form of strict or absolute responsibility for environmental norms should be developed further. Here liability is not based on the breach of an obligation by states, but arises independently through general principles of law, equity, sovereign equality or good neighbourliness. International law recognises a human right to a decent, viable or healthy environment.

With the emergence of the environment as an issue of global concern, this has led to the growth of international environmental law. States have the obligations of restraint and control in the use of their territory and in the exploitation of common spaces.

Environmental law has provided the framework for much political and scientific cooperation for measures of economic assistance and distributive equity for the resolution of international disputes and for the adoption and harmonisation of great deal of national environmental law.

C. Role of States in Promoting Environmental Justice

States have the duty to ensure that modes of thinking that encourage discrimination and colonisation are changed and that attitudes that promote equity and global citizenship are promoted.

States should act with awareness of the world as a global community by recognising and fulfilling their obligation with regard to protection of the rights of global citizens. This means that states should include a level of good will in their foreign policy.

Inter-institutional, national and regional coordination is critical to the promotion of positive attitudes. The way forward is to create a mechanism that encourages states to share their environmental legislation and best practice.

8.   Conclusion

In summary these thoughts on environmental ethics demonstrate that, ethics has an important role to play in ensuring sustainability in a contemporary society. However, it has also been pointed out that ethics alone cannot be effective. The idea is to incorporate ethics in all national and international legislation. It has also been identified that there is an urgent need to deal with the major causes of pollution and environmental degradation and these include poverty, rapid population growth, deforestation and wars amongst others.

Degradation has reached such an alarming stage that it is vital to create greater awareness of environmental problems. Hence it is crucial to consider how humans comprehend their relationship between daily practices and thinking and the sustainability of the natural world.

Finally it is affirmed that any deliberate attempt to reach a rational and enduring state of equilibrium by planned measures, rather than by chance or catastrophe, must ultimately be founded on the basic change of values and goals at individual, national and global levels.

Notes

[1] See BC Pattern, 'Environs: Relativistic Elementary Practical for Ecology', *The American Naturalist*, Vol. 119, 1982, pp. 179-219.

[2] This was noted in S Hanna & M Munasinghe (eds), *Property Rights and the Environment: Social and Ecological Issues*, Beijer Institute of Ecological Economics and The World Bank, Washington DC, 1995, p. 3. We also need to develop the changes proposed by Arrow et al. quick enough to protect our rapidly dwindling global resources for future generations. Arrow et al., 'Economic Growth, Carrying Capacity, and the Environment', *Science,* Vol. 268, 1995, pp. 520-521.

[3] R Baron & W Graziano, *Social Psychology*, Holt Rinehart and Winston, 1991.

[4] ibid.

[5] Allport sets out a definition of attitude in social psychological writing. See GW Allport 'Attitudes' *Handbook of Social Psychology,* CM Murchison (ed), Clark University Press, Worchester, M.A., 1985, p. 810.

[6] See J Palmer & P Neal, *The Handbook of Environmental Education*, Routledge, London, 1994, p. 268.

[7] SK Jacobson, MD McDuff & MC Monroe, *Conservation Education and Outreach Techniques*, Oxford University Press, Oxford, 2006, pp. 25-40.

[8] LA Lefton, *Psychology*, Allyn and Bacon Inc, London, (3rd edition), 1985.

[9] Baron & Graziano, op.cit., pp. 55-60. See also JS Eccles, 'Control Versus Autonomy During Early Adolescence', *Journal of Social Issues,* Vol. 47(4), 1991, pp. 53-68.

[10] BA Day & MC Monroe (eds), *Environmental Education and Communication for a Sustainable World: Handbook for International*

Practitioners, Academy for Educational Development, Washington D.C., 2000.

[11] Indigenous knowledge is broadly defined here: See Hanna & Munasinghe, op.cit., p.7.

[12] ibid, p. 21.

[13] This was cited by BS Nantono, *Environmental Attitudes, Awareness and Participation in Primary Teachers Colleges in Uganda: A Case Study of Three Teachers Colleges.* Unpublished Master's Thesis, Makerere University, Kampala Uganda, p. 113.

[14] F Berkes & C Folke, *Linking Social and Ecological Systems for Resilience and Sustainability.* Background paper and framework prepared for the workshop *Property Rights and the Performance of Natural Resource System*, August 29, 1994, Stockholm, Sweden.

[15] See Hanna & Munasinghe, op.cit., p. 22.

[16] G Hardin's article explains this: G Hardin, 'The Tragedy of the Commons', *Science*, Vol. 162, 1968, pp. 1243-1248.

[17] Thomas Hobbes is an example of moralists who concentrated on man's native egoism to deal effectively with man's insatiate greed: *Collier's Encyclopaedia*, Vol. 9, Macmillan Educational Company, New York, 1989, p. 344.

[18] Aristotle's arguments were in agreement with Jean Bodin but against Machiavelli. Machiavelli's proposal was that the state is judged by the effectiveness of its policies: ibid.

[19] See A Brennan, 'Environmental Ethics', *Stanford Encyclopaedia of Philosophy*, 2008, Viewed on the 3 July 2009, <http://plato.stanford.edu/entries/ethics-environmental/>.

[20] ibid. See also W Grey 'A Critique of Deep Ecology', *Journal of Applied Philosophy*, Vol. 3(2), 1986, pp. 211-216.

[21] In addition to the *Stanford Encyclopaedia*, op.cit., see also, KJ Warren, 'Feminism and Ecology: Making Connections', *Environmental Ethics*, Vol. 9(1), 1987, pp. 3-20. This is also illustrated in V Plumwood, *Feminism and the Mastery of Nature*, Routledge, London, 1993, chapter 7.

[22] HLA Hart, 'Positivism and the Separation of Law and Morals', *Harvard Law Review*, Vol. 71, 1958, pp. 593-529.

[23] For a detailed account of intrinsic value see J O'Neill, 'The Varieties of Intrinsic Value', *Monist,* Vol 75, 1992, pp. 119-137.

[24] He suggests that our well being is dependent upon a sustainable environment. See J Passmore, *Man's Responsibility for Nature,* Duckworth, London, (2nd edition), 1980.

[25] W Friedman, *Legal Theory*, Columbia University Press, New York, (5th edition), 1967, p. 26.

[26] ibid.

[27] ibid.

[28] ibid, p.30.

[29] This is considered further by Jessup in this volume: B Jessup, 'Investing the Law with an Environmental Ethic: Using an Environmental Justice Theory for Change' in *Environmental Law, Ethics & Governance*, E. Techera (ed.), Inter-Disciplinary Press, Oxford, 2010.

Bibliography

Allport, G.W., 'Attitudes'. *Handbook of Social Psychology*. C.M. Murchison (ed), Clark University Press, Worchester, M.A., 1985.

Arrow, K., Bolin, B., Costanza, R., Dasgupta, P., Folke, C., Holling, C.S., Jansson, B.O., Levin, S., Maler, K-G., Perrings, C. & Pimentel, D., 'Economic Growth, Carrying Capacity and the Environment'. *Science*. Vol. 268, 1995. pp. 520–521.

Baron, R.M. & Graziano, W.G., *Social Psychology*. Holt, Rinehart and Winston Inc., Chicago, 1991.

Berkes, F. & Folke, C., *Linking Social and Ecological Systems for Resilience and Sustainability*. Background paper and framework prepared for the workshop *Property Rights and the Performance of Natural Resource System*, Stockholm, Sweden, August 29, 1994.

Berkes, F., Folke, C. & Godgil, M., *Traditional Ecological Knowledge, Biodiversity, Resilience and Sustainability*. Beijer International Institute of Ecological Economies, Beijer Discussion Paper Series No. 31, 1993.

Birnie, P.W. & Boyle, A.E., *International Law and the Environment*. Clarendon Press, Oxford, 1992.

Brennan, A., 'Environmental Ethics'. *Stanford Encyclopaedia of Philosophy*. 2008, Viewed on the 3 July 2009, <http://plato.stanford.edu/entries/ethics-environmental/>.

Collier's Encyclopaedia. Macmillan Educational Company, New York, 1989.

Day, B.A. & Monroe, M.C., *Environmental Education and Communication for a Sustainable World: Handbook for International Practitioners*. Academy for Educational Development, Washington D.C., 2000.

Eccles, J.S., 'Control Versus Autonomy During Early Adolescence'. *Journal of Social Issues*. Vol. 47(4), 1991, pp. 53-68.

Friedmann, W., *Legal Theory*. Columbia University Press, New York, (5th edition), 1967.

Grey, W., 'A Critique of Deep Ecology'. *Journal of Applied Philosophy*. Vol. 3(2), 1986, pp. 211-216.

Hanna, S. & Munasinghe, M. (eds), *Property Rights and the Environment. Social and Ecological Issues*. The Beijer institute of Ecological Economics and The World Bank, Washington DC, 1995.

Hardin, G., 'The Tragedy of the Commons'. *Science*. Vol. 162, 1968, pp. 1243-1248.

Hart, H.L.A., 'Positivism and the Separation of Law and Morals'. *Harvard Law Review*. Vol. 71, 1958, pp. 593-529.

Hegel, G.W.F., *Philosophy of Right*. trans. Knox, T.M., Oxford University Press, Oxford, 1967, (first published by the Clarendon Press, 1952).

Hjort, A. & Salin, M., *Ecology and Politics: Environmental Stress and Security in Africa*. Scandinavian Institute of African Studies, Uppsala, 1980.

Jacobson, S.K., McDuff, M.D. & Monroe, M.C., *Conservation Education and Outreach Techniques*. Oxford University Press, Oxford, 2006.

Jessup, B., 'Investing the Law with an Environmental Ethic: Using an Environmental Justice Theory for Change'. *Environmental Law, Ethics & Governance*. Techera, E. (ed.), Inter-Disciplinary Press, Oxford, 2010.

Kelsen, H., *Introduction to the Problems of Legal Theory*. trans. B. Litschewski-Paulson & S. Paulson, Clarendon Paperbacks Oxford University Press, 2002 (first published 1934).

Lefton, L.A., *Psychology*. Allyn and Bacon, London, (3rd edition), 1985.

Miller, J. & Tyler, G., *Living in the Environment*. Wadsworth Publishing Company, Belmont, California, 1979.

Munroe, R.D. & Lammers, J.G., *Environmental Protection and Sustainable Development: Legal Principles and Recommendations Adopted by the Experts Group on Environmental Law of the World Commission on Environment and Development*. Graham & Trotman/Martinus Nijhoff Publishers, London/Dordrecht, 1987.

Nantono, B.S., *Environmental Attitudes, Awareness and Participation in Primary Teacher's Colleges in Uganda: A Case Study of Three Teachers Colleges*. Unpublished Master's Thesis. Makerere University, Kampala Uganda.

O'Neill, J., 'The Varieties of Intrinsic Value'. *Monist*. Vol. 75, 1992, pp. 119-137.

Palmer, J. & Neal, P., *The Handbook of Environmental Education*. Routledge, London, 1994.

Passmore, J., *Man's Responsibility for Nature*. Duckworth, London, (2nd edition), 1980.

Pattern, B.C., 'Environs: Relativistic Elementary Particles for Ecology'. *The American Naturalist*. Vol. 119, 1982, pp. 179-219.

Plumwood, V., *Feminism and the Mastery of Nature*. Routledge, London, 1999.

Southgate, D. & Desinger, J. (eds), *Sustainable Development in the Third World*. West View Press, Boulder, 1987.

Steiger, H., et al., 'The Fundamental Right to a Decent Environment'. *Trends in Environmental Policy and Law*. Bothe, M. (ed), IUCN, Gland, 1980.

Warren, K.J., 'Feminism and Ecology: Making Connections'. *Environmental Ethics*. Vol. 9(1), 1987, pp. 3-20.

Harriet Nalukenge, Grad ICSA, is a lawyer working as a state attorney in the Ministry of Justice and Constitutional Affairs of the republic of Uganda. Her major role is to defend the government in courts of law. She is involved in human rights advocacy and she writes for *New Vision* a local newspaper in Uganda on pertinent legal issues especially women's rights, democracy and the environment.

Investing the Law with an Environmental Ethic: Using an Environmental Justice Theory for Change

Brad Jessup

Abstract

The adoption of the concept and theory of sustainability by domestic law has not garnered an environmental ethic nor resulted in meaningful changes to legal, political, cultural and community institutions. As a consequence, the law remains incapable of attaining environmental improvements for the benefit of humans and other species. Present day environmental law is still primarily concerned with protecting property interests and upholding a narrow view of responsible government. Further, the law still characterises and purports to protect the environment as divisible components. This chapter argues that introducing a broad and multi-faceted theory of environmental justice drawn from environmental philosophy into the law would redress the environmental ethical deficit in the law. In particular, the chapter shows how an environmentally just legal system would be reformed with a focus on environmental assessment, pollution control, and species preservation laws.

Key Words: Environmental ethics, environmental justice, environmental law, environmental assessment, pollution control, species conservation, participation, recognition, distributional justice.

*****

1. Introduction

The many laws that collectively make up domestic environmental laws are diverse in scope and source. They are drawn from archaic judicial principles of common and public law as well as being designed by modern legislatures ordinarily in response to experienced environmental harm and rarely proactively to ward off predicted environmental problems. Due to their breadth of origin there is a lack of a uniform objective within domestic environmental laws. Rather, hybrid and paradoxical moralities and philosophies underpin them. Environmental laws represent and reflect a mix of social and environmental values: from those values based in economics and private property to those in science, ecosystem and human health.[1]

In recent years the concept of sustainable development and the precautionary principle have been popularised within policy and introduced into statute. Meanwhile, the importance of biological diversity has been understood by law-makers, and a human-environment rights agenda has slowly risen to attention. These trends have resulted in the foundations of domestic environmental laws in common law countries shifting, though only marginally. Environmental laws still are directed first and foremost to protect property interests, regulate polluting activities, conserve species in reserves, and oversee and purport to guide administrative decisions about land uses that might affect ecosystems. Most judges, legislatures and executives remain ignorant of an environmental ethic. In matters relating to the environment they are still principally guided by pragmatism, opportunism, and tradition, not environmentalism.

The experience in Australia shows that the law is lacking an environmental ethic, but can and should be directed by an overarching principle of environmental justice and could promote community behavioural change. This investment of the law with an ethic long familiar to environmental philosophers and social scientists could be achieved in a number of ways. These include by investigating how a greater consideration of notions of access and participation could improve environmental assessment laws and processes, how principles of ecological justice could advance species conservation laws, and how ideals about avoiding environmental discrimination can further shape pollution control laws. This chapter will explore each of these aspects within a framework devised by environmental philosopher David Schlosberg.[2]

2.   The State of Australian Environmental Laws, the Problems with Sustainability, and a Need for an Environmental Ethic

Australian governments and judges are still grappling with what sustainability means.[3] Over the past twenty years in particular the concept of ecological sustainable development, with its twinned principles of precaution and equity across generations,[4] has infiltrated environmental laws and policies. They have been inserted into purpose sections of Acts and used as benchmarks against which government decisions are made.[5] Not much, though, has changed. The precautionary principle has been misunderstood and poorly applied,[6] there are no celebrated cases or decisions in Australia that have halted developments due to concern for future generations, and at best sustainability has been used to apply a triple-bottom-line assessment to proposed developments.[7] Development laws still invariably approve development activities, environmental impact assessment laws do not halt controversial projects,[8] pollution control laws license polluting industry just as before,[9] and biodiversity conservation laws have overseen continued species threats and habitat loss.[10]

There have been glimpses of some progress in climate cases in Australia where planning tribunals have had regard to climate adaptation and, implicitly, intergenerational equity concerns by refusing to permit some coastal developments.[11] However, energy-intensive and coal mining projects with clear and significant increases in greenhouse gas emissions have not been stopped.[12] Concurrently, 'greener' judicial interpretations of laws have been unambiguously overturned on appeal[13] or clarified by parliament cautious that further judicial activism might mean that the laws be used to prohibit potentially harmful activities - and as a corollary become more capable of protecting the environment.[14]

There is no discernible environmental ethic in Australia's environmental laws. Rather, the many laws that collectively make up Australia's environmental protection, biodiversity conservation and land use planning laws are diverse in scope and source. There is no universal objective that balances human and non-human interests.[15] They are drawn from historic principles of tort and property and fundamental constitutional principles of responsible government. In all instances human and proprietary interests are afforded protection and access to the courts while ecological interests do not in themselves have a voice within the law. This is despite the passage of nearly forty years since Christopher Stone advocated that non-human aspects of nature should have standing before the courts through the agency of concerned individuals and groups.[16]

As long as there have been parliaments there have been statutes that regulate human relationships with their surroundings. In Australia, the earliest forms of environmental laws were laws that allocated property interests and reserved lands, mostly for human recreation. It was not until the 1970s that Australian parliaments passed or amended statutes that articulated a concern for environmental protection.[17] Many statutes from that time persist while more have been introduced since. As the decades passed these statutes became more sophisticated and complex as law-makers grappled with community environmental concerns, politics and the unending pursuit of development and growth, albeit sustainable. Legislative purposes are now more directed at preservation, rather than simply being focused on resource use or regulation, and have begun to trial ways of giving effect to the principles of ecological sustainable development. Further, in Australia standing rules for environmental groups have been relaxed[18] and lower standards of proof have been adopted for some environmental offences.[19] Community groups in some jurisdictions have rights to enforce laws[20] and a limited, though rarely used, power to prosecute polluters.[21] They have rights to participate in decision-making processes and to access information.[22] These laws, however, are not universal. The environmental credentials are not matched in other laws and there is no overarching philosophy that has led to their enactment, or that can be used as a benchmark for evaluating their implementation and interpretation.

3.   An Environmental Ethic for the Law
Agyeman[23] argues that green theorists and professional environmentalists have succeeded in refining the concept of sustainability to advance a conservation agenda and to impose an environmental platform on

communities.[24] Agyeman particularly identifies Dobson, whose work employs the terminology 'environmental sustainability', which Dobson conceives as having a broader and less anthropocentric scope than the concept of 'sustainable development'. Within the minority, high-income, and usually high-polluting countries of the world, given their wealth and past and ongoing degradation of ecosystems, this reconceptualisation of sustainability by environmentalists is understandable and defendable. As Dobson articulates in his three types of environmental sustainability the goal of the concept is the maintenance of the natural environment.[25]

The experience throughout the world is that, despite the trend towards the promotion of 'environmental sustainability', environmental outcomes have not generally been improved.[26] In Australia, the adoption of the principle of ecological sustainable development has not modified environmental laws in a way that gives pre-eminent importance to the protection of the environment over other socio-political concerns. The status quo is clearly illustrated in the legal saga surrounding the Wielanga forest in Tasmania. In that case a legal obligation to create a system of reserves to protect nominated threatened species in furtherance of ecological sustainable development was interpreted and later clarified by the Australian and Tasmanian governments as not requiring the protection of species at all.[27] The existence of ineffective reserves was enough to fulfil the legal obligation. At best sustainability has lead to incremental and piecemeal environmental improvements. In practice the meaning of sustainability has been contested[28] and in particular it has been simplified into a triple-bottom-line assessment tool.[29] Due to these features the principle of sustainable development as it is currently used is unlikely to advance environmental laws in a way that promotes environmental protection and conservation, which sometimes must be at the expense of development. It is doubtful it could be the model to promote the behavioural change needed. In searching for an environmental ethic for environmental laws, we must look beyond 'sustainable development' and its various iterations.

The principle of sustainable development was primarily intended to be used as an empowering human development philosophy in the majority world,[30] rather than be used as a justification for a continuation of the minority world's development fixation. In its originally conceived form sustainable development has an ongoing relevance, especially when understood as a mechanism to pursue justice for communities.[31] Agyeman[32] argues that sustainable development needs to be reframed within an environmental justice philosophy so that it more adequately responds to the needs and concerns of the less advantaged. In high-income countries like Australia it is also time to reconsider the benchmark used to evaluate environmental performance, particularly of environmental laws and activities approved by legislation or the courts.

Some of Agyeman's 'just sustainability' ideas could be applied in the minority world to concurrently advance the livelihoods of the least advantaged and devise a benchmark to evaluate environmental performance. Instead of using a concept that is solely anthropocentric such as is imagined by Dobson[33], however, any such test for environmental performance or evaluation could include both anthropocentric and ecocentric philosophies[34] and with them an environmental ethic. Decisions would therefore be more mindful of both human and non-human interests and could not simply be based on majority utilitarian preferences at the expense of non-conventional or non-economic concerns.

Any new overarching environmental principle or readjusted version of sustainable development should also be more environmentally democratic[35] allowing it to be advocated and advanced by the community, not just the government and business world with their shared mastery of slippery language. This would mean that there is a greater role for deliberation, a prioritisation of voices dissenting to potentially harmful activities and a respect for non-human parts of the environment. Further, a more environmentally democratic framework for environmental law would encourage openness, transparency, collectivity and fairness within environmental and governmental institutions. While some of these features have been attributed to the principle of sustainable development,[36] they have not always been central in its application in environmental laws.

4.   A Concept of Environmental Justice for Environmental Law

Much has been written and said about the relationships between the law and justice since Aristotelian times.[37] It is not important to revisit these commentaries here other than to note that the discipline and institution of law is fundamentally concerned with the maintenance and delivery of justice. The notion of 'environmental justice', however, is largely absent from global and domestic legal systems and jurisprudence. The closest the institutions and the profession have come to recognise a notion of environmental justice is to identify and categorise those laws that promote fair environmental processes and that can be used to avert disproportionate environmental damage on human communities.[38] This marginal progress is despite the development of the concept of environmental justice over more than 30 years[39] and its presence in United States policy and advocacy since the 1990s.[40] Perhaps it has been because of the narrow focus of the environmental justice movement.[41] The movement's concerns have primarily centred on the distribution of environmentally harmful industry and land use.[42] The limited adoption of environmental justice into law might also be because the principle has been treated as having relevance only in the United States, where distributive environmental injustice in environmental policy-making and land-use planning decisions has been researched and successfully demonstrated.[43] Midley's[44] work suggests that the narrowing of justice theories into a social contract model of human relations gives little scope for its application to non-human entities. It is also possible that the concept of environmental justice has been overlooked or denied by the law because the concept has been so closely aligned with those people often ignored by, and powerless to act within, a largely culturally homogenous system devised, implemented, and maintained by the socially privileged.[45]

A wide and inclusive interpretation of environmental justice[46] has the benefit of embracing conceptual deviation[47] and overcoming the reluctance to adopt distributive environmental justice notions into law. In fact, despite the unwillingness of some academics to 'move beyond the distributive paradigm'[48] and towards a plural,[49] more abstract and universal[50] model, the concept of environmental justice has been explored, theorised and expanded by others.[51] It is now capable of broader application and suitable for use as a framework principle to guide and assess environmental laws either as a stand-alone principle or as a component of an environmentally just sustainable development principle.

In its expansive understanding environmental justice encompasses rights of access, information and participation of humans, recognition of non-human interests of nature, and concern for the fair distribution of environmental harm and environmental services. These are all features that can be incorporated into a system of environmental laws that deals with land use regulation, the assessment of potentially harmful and locally controversial developments, pollution control and licensing, and the review of administrative decisions.

Through an analysis of historical and contemporary writings on justice, environmental justice and ecological justice, Schlosberg[52] provides an interconnected definition of environmental justice. While he is not alone in trying to further explain and theorise a broad concept of environmental justice,[53] Schlosberg's work is comprehensive, deeply grounded in well-established and accepted theory, and well-suited for application to legal scholarship.

In Schlosberg's view[54], environmental justice has four aspects. The first aspect is distribution. As mentioned previously, this aspect is the most commonly understood form of environmental justice: the fair distribution of environmental harm and goods. It remains the focus of the environmental justice movement, which is concerned with overcoming the nexus between minority and disadvantaged communities with polluting and contaminating industry and activities. It is drawn from distributional justice theories, which are overwhelmingly anthropocentric and afford little scope for inclusion of the non-human world. It shares similarities with current equal opportunity laws, which create civil penalties for discriminating against humans on the basis of a characteristic,[55] and which were one of the stimuli for the formation of the environmental justice movement.[56] While these laws do not at present ordinarily provide grounds for complaint of discrimination on the basis of location or social status, they do so on the basis of race, ethnicity and parental or marital status; all of which have been linked with higher exposure to environmental pollution.

The second aspect, recognition,[57] is much more capable of incorporating ecocentric values within a broad concept of environmental justice. As well as ensuring that all human interests are recognised within decision-making and environmental distributions rather than being dominated or oppressed by institutions like the law, this aspect of environmental justice can recognise non-human aspects of nature as having interests, and of requiring preservation actions to maintain ecological integrity. It draws on the theory of ecological justice[58], is concerned with respect for humans and non-humans, an end of marginalisation, stereotyping, denigration, and invisibility, and has obvious connections with standing doctrines in law. It was these common law doctrines that Stone challenged in his seminal work[59] in the 1970s. However, at common law the rules remain deeply instrumental and anthropocentric - with individuals, corporations or groups having to show a proprietary or personal and specific interest, as distinct from an intellectual or emotional interest, before the court will entertain their application.[60]

Recognition is an important conceptual link between substantive distributional justice and procedural participatory justice, which is the third aspect of Schlosberg's[61] concept of environmental justice. Without recognition any participation in decisions that influence distribution will be too narrow or inherently biased with positions assumed and human participants and non-human values typecast, ignored or absent from deliberations. Deliberative and environmental democracy theorists[62] have explored the appropriate nature of participation. The participation must occur early, be equally funded, inclusive, deliberative rather than informative, and contribute to democratic decisions. Non-human participation would need to occur through human agents. This aspect has strong similarities with environmental legal discourses on access to justice, with a broader outlook than standing rules and wider application to procedure and non-judicial decision-making. The discourses were recently translated by the European Community into the Aarhus *Convention on Access to Information, Public Participation in Decision-Making and Access to Justice in Environmental Matters* to redress the 'green democratic deficit'[63] within European Union decision-making. In practice the Convention has not yet shaken the conservative and orthodox view on matters of administrative law, nor have the vesting of 'rights' in the community made debates and decisions of importance to environmental groups more open and participatory while institutional and environmental value barriers persist.[64]

The fourth aspect is capabilities. Schlosberg[65] argues that environmental justice should build capabilities in individuals and groups. Capabilities would generally be a by-product of just treatment and outcomes. In the legal field they would have particular relevance at the institutional and advocate level. Participation is often the mechanism through which capabilities are built or strengthened. Capabilities are the things that humans need to function and flourish politically, emotionally, physically, socially, economically, and spiritually. They are about putting rights and opportunities to use.[66] In environmental law, they would include gaining respect from decision-makers and respectful treatment between, and equalising treatment of, development proponents and opponents, having an ability to present alternative perspectives to decision-makers, being protected from environmental degradation, and accessing, learning and using advocacy and activism skills, and community and affiliation building. It is the work of Sen[67] in particular that provides the theoretical basis for this aspect of environmental justice. Schlosberg[68] argues that capabilities, and therefore the concept of environmental justice, can be communal as well as individual. Capabilities can also attach to the ecosystem. At the ecosystem level capabilities are seen as facilitating ecological health and system and process integrity.

According to Schlosberg,[69] environmental justice must be afforded to both the individual and the community. Further, within an environmental legal system in an environmental democracy its application would be universal, not just associated with individuals and groups within the environmental justice movement. The principle would act to counter the techno-economic approach to development within existing liberal democratic structures. Its potential would only be realised with a shift in environmental power, an embrace of deliberate forms of decision making, an acceptance of non-human environmental values in the policy framework, a reassessment of meanings of fairness, impartiality and equity to include ecosystem values, and a commitment to maintain ecosystem integrity.

5.   A Legal Reformation

Rowe[70] argues that environmental law could shift, and only needs to shift marginally, to adopt and reflect an environmental justice ethic. Already environmental law deals with matters of distribution and location through laws of nuisance, land use planning, the regulation of transboundary movements of waste and pollution control. Environmental law already imposes equitable standards through the pricing of environmental damage and the implementation of the polluter pays rationale. The law also includes the infrequently used doctrine of the public trust, which theoretically can be employed to protect anthropocentric environmental concerns.[71] As mentioned above, the European Community has also demonstrated a way to empower the public.

A concept of environmental justice could be incorporated into environmental legal systems through legislation. Like the concept of ecological sustainable development, as a first measure it could be included into objects of Acts and nominated as a relevant consideration in the many regulated decision-making processes in Australia. If environmental justice is understood as being broad, multi-faceted and directed at both human wellbeing and ecological integrity then advancements in conservation and protection could be realised, most likely in an ad hoc manner as a second wave of greening of environmental laws following the current sustainable development law agenda. Such an approach would not, however, universalise environmental justice or provide an overarching environmental ethic framework that domestic legal systems generally lack. More would be required.

One benefit of the concept of environmental justice as an environmental ethic in domestic legal systems is that it has a deeply philosophical foundation, avoids some of the vagueness of the principles of sustainable development, intergenerational equity and precaution, and the four aspects of environmental justice described above can be characterised as rights in terminology readily recognisable by the law. There is scope, therefore, to have an Act of Parliament, similar to or within a human rights charter. The consequence of such an action would be to elevate environmental laws from being constantly subject to administrative ignorance or discretion and legislative amendment and repeal to being inviolable.[72] Such an Act would subject all governmental action to the concept of environmental justice and require the administration, implementation and interpretation of legislation to comply with environmental justice standards as well as guaranteeing features of an environmentally democratic society – like deliberation, access to courts, rights to advocate on behalf of a potentially affected ecosystem, and funding for environmental advocacy. If the law does have an endogenous effect, then an environmental justice charter could lead to community behavioural and value change. The United States Clinton Administration went part of the way towards doing this with its Executive Order on Environmental Justice,[73] which required all federal agencies to consider distributive environmental justice in their operations. The environmental justice movement has also developed 'principles of environmental justice' that articulate qualities of an environmentally just society.[74] The contribution of the international law community in this regard is also starting to become apparent with a discernible climate justice discourse aligned with the international law principle of common but differentiated responsibilities.[75]

Aside from investing the law with an environmental justice ethic though a legislative reformation, there is also the possibility of cultivating the legal system to be environmentally just and demonstrating how an environmental ethic will enhance justice as understood by the existing system. The works of Hajer[76] and Sabatier[77] demonstrate how coalitions could shape legal understanding through discourse and advocacy. The environmental justice movement could be joined by environmental ethicists, environmental groups, environmental democrats and participation advocates, just as Harvey urges when he writes of environmental justice being 'transcendent', 'universal' and 'radicalise[d]'[78] beyond its distributive origins. If this were to happen then a broader environmental justice discourse would gain a prominence that it does not have: even in the United States where advocacy and discussion has promoted the distributive aspect of environmental justice.

Receptiveness to environmental justice arguments will of course depend on the environmental values and philosophies of policy and decision-makers. Jurists, particularly in Australia, have a reputation for being deferential to orthodoxy, unreceptive to legal arguments based on novel rights,[79] still struggle with understanding the principle of ecological sustainable development,[80] and have not yet grappled with submissions drawn from environmental ethics. Based on a similar experience in the United Kingdom, Lord Woolf questions whether judges there are 'environmentally myopic'.[81] The conclusion that Lord Woolf reaches in asking how to get judges to interpret and enforce environmental laws in a way that advances environmental conservation and protection is that environmental laws should be interpreted and enforced by a specialist environmental body.[82] The experience in New South Wales, where the Land and Environment Court has heard environmental and planning cases for almost 30 years[83] and has been the leader in the development of environmental jurisprudence in Australia,[84] gives hope that the judicial branch of government can be skilled to approach its task with an environmental ethic if the court has a focused environmental law jurisdiction.

6.   Access and Participation in Environmental Assessment

There are three areas of domestic environmental and planning laws where the adoption of the concept of environmental justice, or specific aspects of environmental justice, is compelling and would help environmental law achieve existing objectives. The first is environmental assessment laws. The purposes and processes of environmental assessment have been analysed and theorised in depth elsewhere.[85] They include rigorous investigations, participatory inquiries, transparent decisions and minimisation of environmental harm.

So how would the concept of environmental justice, whether imposed on decision makers through legislative force or influenced by a co-ordinated community effort change environmental assessment laws? First, an environmentally just assessment regime would prioritise impartial deliberation and participation over proponent-designed and led consultation and information dissemination. Individuals and community groups would be put on the same financial, procedural and expert footing as government agents and the proponent. They would be recognised as being capable of contributing and their capabilities to contribute would be supported. Individuals and community groups with concerns about adverse distributive effects of any future project and those with concerns about the impacts on the ecosystem would be identified, invited and involved in devising project details, specifying the investigation breadth, evaluating preliminary findings and directing further scientific and social research. As provided by the Aarhus Convention, information would be easily accessible. The government would provide funding, which would allow individuals and groups involved in the assessment process to engage lawyers and experts to assist them offer alternative views to those provided by the more powerful government and proponent spokespeople. With early and meaningful deliberation, public inquiries, which in Australia are almost always adversarial, costly and time consuming, could be discarded.

Secondly, environmental assessment would become an approval process rather than simply be an assessment process, as it most commonly is in Australia. This change would recognise the contribution of all parties to the process and inexorably link the process with the outcome. In recognition of the non-human parts of the ecosystem, if a project is assessed as having any threats to ecosystem process or integrity it could not be approved. Human agents would not be able to trade-away the interests of the non-human world in the assessment process as they currently do with the process of off-setting.[86] Such trading-away would undermine the capabilities and the recognition of ecosystems. Further, approvals would not be given that produce distributional environmental injustice unless those effects have been canvassed and understood by the community. As Smith[87] notes, governments must make decisions about environmental policies and proposed projects and they cannot always please everyone, particularly because consensus infrequently arises from deliberation. Hence, occasionally an outcome that results in an unjust distribution of environmental harm may still arise in the application of an environmentally just law. There may be compelling reasons for condoning that distribution. For instance there may be locally desirable advantages like services, utilities and economic benefits or no alternative for a locally undesirable development. The goal of a deliberative democracy is that the decision is supported, and capable of being explained and justified, by an environmental assessment.

Finally, decisions made by government officials would need to be capable of review by an impartial specialist court or tribunal to satisfy the recognition and participation aspects of the concept of environmental justice. Standing would be open, including all groups and all human agents of the ecosystem and not just restricted to those individuals with personal interests affected. The approach included in the Australian *Environment Protection and Biodiversity Conservation Act 1999* (Cth)[88] would be broadened even further. While there is ongoing commentary, particularly by environmental groups, about the limitations of judicial review and the preference for merits review as a tool to achieve better decisions for the environment,[89] an environmentally just and democratic form of review would not necessarily entail full merits review. Unending challenges to decisions does not enhance participation and undermines the respect for and recognition of the proponent of an approved project and merits review acts to divest decision-makers of responsibility for making just decisions.

An appropriate legal framework, like the entrenchment of environmental justice principles, would obviate the need for merits review. Further, environmental justice could accompany 'natural justice' as a new ground of a more accessible, affordable and cost-neutral judicial review. An environmentally just legal system with concerns for participation and capability-building could not oversee government agencies pursuing community groups for legal costs.[90] Nor could it allow judges to decline injunctive relief where the possibility of damage to ecological processes or ecological integrity is likely to arise from alleged illegal or unapproved development.

7.   Ecological Justice and Species Conservation Laws

In addition to broadening standing rules to permit human agents to advocate on behalf of non-human species and systems, and avoiding ecological trade-off, the ecological justice input into an environmentally just legal system would have application to species conservation laws. Schlosberg's recognition aspect of environmental justice would be afforded to the whole ecosystem and communities, not just endangered species, as an acknowledgment of the contribution of biological diversity to ecosystem integrity and resilience.[91] Adopting the language of the New Zealand *Resource Management Act 1991*, laws would be directed at sustaining ecological function.[92] However, unlike that Act the function would be preserved across all scales and for the intrinsic purpose of retaining ecosystems rather than for the anthropocentric and instrumental purpose of preserving 'natural resources'. The approach adopted in some states in Australia to reserve river water flows for the environment,[93] for the benefit of the ecosystem rather than for human benefit, also provides a model for an ecologically just legal system.

An environmentally just domestic legal system would not permit proposals that involve the degradation of ecosystems unless proponents could prove that the activity would not threaten species or ecosystem integrity and health, which is similar to the approach in the United States' *Endangered Species Act of 1973*.[94] The burden of proof would be reversed compared to the current situation in Australia. In Australia, the question ordinarily asked in any approval process is how much development can occur, and then be approved, before already endangered communities or species become further endangered. Invariably projects are assessed individually rather than collectively or mindful of cumulative ecological impacts. Non-endangered species are not considered.[95] The capacity of the ecosystem and species to sustain ongoing health would be enhanced through positive obligations in legislation to maintain species and ecosystem integrity. This differs from the usual current approach of prohibiting activities that might threaten or further endanger nominated species or communities or of simply closing off systems in parks.

8.   Environmental Discrimination and Pollution Control Laws

The most obvious and powerful changes to the law, to make them environmentally just, need to be made to pollution laws that limit distributional environmental injustice and that build capabilities of individuals and groups to oppose or prevent pollution or contamination. A starting point would be to apply the same standing principles for environmental assessment and administrative review of decisions to the review of grants of licences and the enforcement of licence conditions and pollution control laws. Any individual or community should have the right to challenge approvals and to enforce compliance with the law. The civil enforcement regime under the Victorian *Planning and Environment Act 1987*, where any person for any reason can apply to a specialist tribunal to halt and remediate unlawful development,[96] could provide the appropriate model. A broadened New South Wales *Protection of the Environment Operations Act 1997,* with an unfettered capacity to initiate public enforcement and prosecution[97] and with government funding provided for legal representation,[98] would also go some way to making pollution control laws more environmentally just. Such moderate reforms would help build community capabilities to enforce rights and would more fairly allocate access to legal expertise.

In order to avoid environmental discrimination in the location of polluting industry, pollution control laws should be connected with land use planning laws. In most Australian jurisdictions this is the case with planning and pollution approvals considered concurrently. Zone plans, however, could be revised with a conscious effort at fairly distributing planned locations of potentially harmful activities. This would ensure that communities can only ever host a limited number of clusters of harmful activities, rather than some communities bearing the environmental problems associated with multiple disturbing land uses. This revision would need to be done on a regional rather than local scale in order to most fairly distribute burdens across urban and rural districts of connected communities. As a change initiated and promulgated by government it should also be subject to the overarching charter of environmental justice that would prevent government decisions from unfairly burdening communities.

9.   Conclusion

If it is agreed that environmental protection and conservation are worthy environmental law objectives whether for human wellbeing or for ecocentric philosophical concerns then we need to reform our domestic environmental legal systems. Reformation is needed because the current sustainable development focus is not supporting conservation and protection approaches. Rather, in many cases the principle of ecological sustainable development is being used to support potentially harmful activities to realise the short-term economic benefits the activity is predicted to generate. Sustainable development, as a concept or theory used in the minority world, lacks an environmental ethic and a clear articulation of its components. To overcome these limitations an environmental justice philosophy could be applied to environmental laws through mandate, collective activism, or by institutional change. Behavioural change could then follow.

Adopting Schlosberg's[99] conceptualisation of environmental justice, a domestic environmental legal system could limit the unfair distribution of environmental harm, recognise human and non-human interests in the law, enable and increase impartial participation and build capabilities and resilience in the human and non-human parts of nature. This can particularly be achieved through a focus on environmental assessment, species conservation and pollution control laws, broadening standing to review decisions and enforce laws, funding environmental litigation and by creating specialised environmental courts.

Notes

[1] See S Fleisher-Trainor, 'Realms of Value: Conflicting Natural Resource Values and Incommensurability', *Environmental Values,* Vol. 15 No. 1, pp. 3-27. Fleisher-Trainor argues that environmental values occur at different realms and are therefore often perceived as being incommensurable.
[2] D Schlosberg, *Defining Environmental Justice: Theories, Movements, and Nature*, Oxford University Press, Oxford, 2007; D Schlosberg, 'Reconceiving Environmental Justice: Global Movements and Political Theories',

Environmental Politics, Vol. 13, No. 3, 2004, pp. 517-540; D Schlosberg, *Environmental Justice and the New Pluralism,* Oxford University Press, Oxford, 1999.

[3] The Australian Capital Territory's Commissioner for the Environment recently re-badged herself the Commissioner for Sustainability and the Environment without articulating what sustainability means. In *Blue Wedges Inc v Minister for the Environment, Heritage and the Arts* (2008) 167 FCR 463 one of the matters for resolution was whether the principle of ecological sustainable development in the *Environment Protection and Biodiversity Conservation Act 1999* (Cth) applies to specific impacts rather than holistic impacts and whether it be applied to social, economic and environmental concerns separately or together.

[4] See the 1992 Intergovernmental Agreement on the Environment and the *Environment Protection and Biodiversity Conservation Act 1999* (Cth).

[5] P Biscoe (Justice), *Ecologically Sustainable Development in New South Wales,* paper delivered on 2 June 2007 at the 5th Worldwide Colloquium of the IUCN Academy of Environmental Law, Paraty, Brazil. See for example the *Environment Protection and Biodiversity Conservation Act 1999* (Cth) and the *Protection of the Environment Administration Act 1991* (NSW) and Commonwealth of Australia, *National Strategy for Ecologically Sustainable Development,* 1992.

[6] See for example *Wildlife Preservation Society of Queensland Proserpine/Whitsunday Branch Inc v Minister for the Environment & Heritage* (2006) 232 ALR 510 and *Telstra Corp Ltd v Hornsby Shire Council* (2006) 67 NSWLR 256.

[7] In the Portland Wind Energy Project, for example, the principle of ecological sustainable development was evaluated on a triple-bottom-line basis. The Project only received an endorsement from the independent assessment panel on the basis of its large economic benefits. These benefits, in the absence of policy support for renewable energy developments at the time, were considered to outweigh adverse local environmental and social concerns.

[8] For example the Macarthur River Mine in the Northern Territory, which proceeded only after executive and parliamentary intervention, the Channel Deepening Project in Victoria, which was approved after a second environmental assessment process, and the Gunns Pulp Mill, which was approved after the proponent withdrew from the environmental assessment process, forcing Commonwealth and Tasmanian governments to retrofit assessment processes.

[9] See for example State of Victoria (Environmental Protection Authority of Victoria), *EPA Annual Report 2008*, p. A8, which shows that works approvals remain relatively constant since 2003.

[10] See for example International Union for Conservation of Nature and Natural Resources, *The IUCN Red List of Threatened Species*, 2009, data version 2009.1, Viewed on 1 August 2009, <http://www.iucnredlist.org>.

[11] See for example *Gippsland Coastal Board v South Gippsland Shire Council* (No 2) [2008] VCAT 1545 (Unreported, DP Gibson & M Potts, 29 August 2008) and *Northcape Properties Pty Ltd v District Council of Yorke Peninsula* [2007] SAERDC 50 (Unreported, C Mosel, 19 September 2007) upheld by *Northcape Properties Pty Ltd v District Council of Yorke Peninsula* [2008] SASC 57 (Unreported, J Debelle, 4 March 2008).

[12] For example *Australian Conservation Foundation v Latrobe City Council* (2004) 140 LGERA 100 and *Wildlife Preservation Society of Queensland Proserpine/Whitsunday Branch Inc v Minister for the Environment & Heritage* (2006) 232 ALR 510.

[13] See for example *Walker v Minister for Planning* (2007) 157 LGERA 124, overturned by *Minister for Planning v Walker* (2008) 161 LGERA 423; *Brown v Forestry Tasmania (No 4)* (2006) 157 FCR 1 overturned by *Forestry Tasmania v Brown* (2007) 167 FCR 34.

[14] For example the insertion of s 527E of the *Environment Protection and Biodiversity Conservation Act 1999* (Cth) through the enactment of the *Environment and Heritage Legislation Amendment Act (No 1) 2006* (Cth) bounded the breadth of 'indirect impacts' raised in *Queensland Conservation Council Inc v Minister for the Environment and Heritage* [2003] FCA 1463 (Unreported, J Kiefel, 19 December 2003) and confirmed in *Minister for the Environment and Heritage v Queensland Conservation Council Inc* (2004) 139 FCR 24. Amendments to the Regional Forests Agreement between the Commonwealth of Australia and the State of Tasmania on 23 February 2007 that nullified the effect of *Brown v Forestry Tasmania (No 4)* (2006) 157 FCR 1.

[15] J Radcliffe, *Green Politics: Dictatorship or Democracy?* Palgrave, Basingstoke, Hampshire and New York, 2002. See particularly Ch. 4 'The Need for an Environmental Ethic'.

[16] C Stone, 'Should Trees have Standing? Toward Legal Rights for Natural Objects', *Should Trees have Standing? And Other Essays on Law, Morals and the Environment*, C Stone (ed), Oxford University Press, Oxford, 1996 (25th anniversary ed), Ch. 1.

[17] The *Environment Protection Act 1970* (Vic), *Wildlife Act 1975* (Vic) and *Environment Effects Act 1978* (Vic) all still exist in Victoria.

[18] *Environment Protection and Biodiversity Conservation Act 1999* (Cth), s 487.

[19] See for example the civil penalty provisions in the *Environment Protection and Biodiversity Conservation Act 1999* (Cth) and in the *Environment Protection Act 1993* (SA).

[20] Most land use planning laws contain such rights. For instance, the *Planning and Environment Act 1987* (Vic), the *Development Act 1993* (SA), and the *Environmental Planning and Assessment Act 1979* (NSW).

[21] In the past five years there has been no reported case of an individual using the public prosecution rights in section 219 of the *Protection of the Environment Operations Act 1997* (NSW).

[22] See for example *Human Rights Act 2004* (ACT), *Charter of Human Rights and Responsibilities Act 2006* (Vic), and *Protection and Public Participation Act 2008* (ACT).

[23] J Agyeman, *Sustainable Communities and the Challenge of Environmental Justice*, New York University Press, New York, 2005.

[24] See A Dobson, *Justice and the Environment: Conceptions of Environmental Sustainability and Dimensions of Social Justice,* Oxford University Press, Oxford, 1998.

[25] Dobson, loc.cit.

[26] Agyeman, loc.cit.

[27] *Forestry Tasmania v Brown* (2007) 167 FCR 34 (especially paras [80] onwards, where the variation to the *Tasmanian Forest Agreement* dated 23 February 2007 is discussed.

[28] See note 1.

[29] See note 4.

[30] W Adams, *Green Development: Environment and Sustainability in the Third World*, Routledge, London, 2001 (2nd ed).

[31] Agyeman, loc.cit. Though on this point Dobson has previously doubting that the concerns of justice and conservation can always be consistent: Dobson, op.cit.

[32] Agyeman, loc.cit.

[33] Dobson, loc. cit.

[34] D Harvey, 'The Environment of Justice', *Living With Nature: Environmental Politics as Cultural Discourse,* F Fischer & M Hajer (eds), Oxford University Press, Oxford, 1999, Ch. 8. For a distinction between anthropocentric and ecocentric philosophies see, for example, R Eckersley, *Environmentalism and Political Theory: Towards an Ecocentric Approach*, UCL Press, London, 1992.

[35] M Mason, *Environmental Democracy*, Earthscan, London, 1999.

[36] J Meadowcroft, 'Participation and Sustainable Development: Modes of Citizen, Community and Organisational Involvement', *Governance for Sustainable Development: The Challenge of Adapting Form to Function,* W Lafferty (ed), Edgar Elgar Press, Cheltenham, 2004, Ch. 6.

[37] For a contemporary reflection on the law and justice writings of Aristotle see A Beever, 'Aristotle on Equity, Law and Justice', *Legal Theory,* Vol. 10, No. 1, 2004, pp. 33-50.

[38] See for example M Gerrard & S Foster (eds), *The Law of Environmental Justice: Theories and Procedures to Address Disproportionate Risks,* American Bar Association, Chicago, 2008 (2nd ed).

[39] L Cole & S Foster, *From the Ground Up: Environmental Racism and the Rise of the Environmental Justice Movement,* New York University Press, New York and London, 2001. See especially Ch. 1 'A History of the Environmental Justice Movement' where the origins of the concept of environmental justice are explored. These origins are traced to academia, the civil rights movement and the increased prevalence and awareness of toxic waste in the United States.

[40] Ibid; C Rechtschaffen & E Gauna (eds), *Environmental Justice: Law, Policy and Regulation,* Carolina Academic Press, Durham, North Carolina, 2003 (2nd ed). The key moments in the formalising of environmental justice in US politics were the 1991 First National People of Colour Environmental Leadership Summit and President Clinton's Executive Order 12898 of 11 February 1994 *Federal Actions to Address Environmental Justice in Minority Populations and Low-Income Populations.*

[41] Schlosberg, 2004, op.cit., p. 529, describes discrete theories of environmental justice, including the theory of distributive justice promoted by the environmental justice movement as 'disappointing' because of their lack of integration.

[42] Dobson, loc.cit.

[43] Cole and Foster, op.cit., Appendix.

[44] M Midley, 'Duties Concerning Island States', R Elliot & A Gare (eds), *Environmental Philosophy*, University of Queensland Press, St Lucia, 1983, pp. 166-181.

[45] K Shrader-Frechette, *Environmental Justice: Creating Equality, Reclaiming Democracy,* Oxford University Press, New York, 2002; Schlosderg, loc.cit.

[46] Schlosberg, op.cit., p. 518, advocates a 'locally grounded, theoretically broad, and plural' notion of environmental justice.

[47] J Callewaert, 'The Multiple and Competing Conceptions of Environmental Justice', *Global Citizenship and Environmental Justice,* T Shallcross & J Robinson (eds), Rodopi Press, Amsterdam, 2006, pp. 21-40.

[48] Schlosberg, 2004, op.cit., p. 531.

[49] Schlosberg, 1999, loc.cit.

[50] Harvery, loc.cit.

[51] Schlosberg, 2007, loc.cit.; Harvey, loc.cit.; Mason, loc.cit.; B Barry, 'Sustainable and Intergenerational Justice', A Dobson (ed), *Fairness and Futurity: Essays on Environmental Sustainability and Social Justice*, Oxford University Press, Oxford, 1999, Ch. 4; N Low & B Gleeson, *Justice, Society and Nature: An Exploration of Political Ecology*, Routledge, London, 1998 (who despite resisting a move from the distributive frame introduced ideas of participatory and ecological justice into a theory of environmental justice).

[52] Schlosberg, 2007, loc.cit.

[53] See note 51.

[54] Schlosberg, 2007, loc.cit.

[55] See for example the *Equal Opportunity Act 1995* (Vic).

[56] Cole & Foster, loc.cit. See particularly the discussion on the Civil Rights Movement.

[57] Schlosberg, 2007, loc.cit.

[58] Low & Gleeson, loc.cit.; K Bosselman, 'Ecological Justice and Law', *Environmental Law for Sustainability*, B Richardson & S Wood (eds), Hart Publishing, Oxford and Portland, Oregon, 2006.

[59] Stone, loc.cit.

[60] M Groves & HP Lee, *Australian Administrative Law: Fundamentals, Principles and Doctrines*, Cambridge University Press, New York, 2007. See also the case of *Australian Conservation Foundation v Commonwealth* (1980) 146 CLR 493.

[61] Schlosberg, 2007, loc.cit.

[62] For example, Mason, loc.cit.; Harvey, loc.cit.

[63] M Lee, *EU Environmental Law: Challenges, Change and Decision-Making*, Hart Publishing, Oxford and Portland, Oregon, 2005, p. 121.

[64] Lee.

[65] Schlosberg, 2007, loc.cit.

[66] Ibid.

[67] A Sen, *Development as Freedom,* Oxford University Press, Oxford, 1999.

[68] Schlosberg, 2007, op.cit.

[69] Ibid.

[70] G Rowe, 'Environmental Justice as an Ethical, Economic and Legal Principle', *Environmental Justice and Market Mechanisms: Key Challenges for Environmental Law and Policy*, B Richardson & K Bosselman (eds), Kluwer Law International, London, 1999, Ch. 4.

[71] T Hoban & R Brooks, *Green Justice: The Environment and the Courts*, Westview Press, Boulder, 1996 (2nd ed). See especially Ch. 12.

[72] D Shelton, 'Environmental Justice in the Postmodern World', *Environmental Justice and Market Mechanisms: Key Challenges for Environmental Law and Policy*, B Richardson & K Bosselman (eds), Kluwer Law International, London, 1999, Ch. 2.

[73] Executive Order 12898 of 11 February 1994 *Federal Actions to Address Environmental Justice in Minority Populations and Low-income Populations*. See also Rechtschaffen & Gauna (eds), loc.cit.

[74] See for example the 'Principles of Environmental Justice' adopted at the People of Colour Environmental Leadership Summit in October 1991 and reproduced in J Agyeman, op.cit, R Bullard & B Evans (eds), *Just Sustainabilities: Development in an Unequal World*, The MIT Press, Cambridge Massachusetts, 2003, Appendix 1.

[75] *Rio Declaration on Environment and Development*, 1992, principle 7; J Brunnée, 'Climate Change, Global Environmental Justice and International Environmental Law', *Environmental Law and Justice in Context*, J Ebbesson & P Okowa (eds), Cambridge University Press, Cambridge, 2009, Ch. 16.

[76] M Hajer, *The Politics of Environmental Discourse: Ecological Modernization and the Policy Process*, Oxford University Press, Oxford, 1995.

[77] P Sabatier, 'Knowledge, Policy Orientated Learning and Policy Change: An Advocacy Coalition Framework', *Knowledge: Creation, Diffusion, Utilization*, Vol. 8, 1987, p 649.

[78] Harvey, op.cit., pp. 183-184.

[79] See for example H Charlesworth, 'The High Court and Human Rights', *Centenary Essays for the High Court of Australia*, P Cane (ed), LexisNexis Butterworths, Sydney, 2004, pp. 356-369.

[80] See *Blue Wedges Inc v Minister for the Environment, Heritage and the Arts* (2008) 167 FCR 463, paras [65] to [89].

[81] H Woolf, *The Pursuit of Justice*, Oxford University Press, Oxford, 2008, Ch. 22.

[82] Ibid, Ch. 22 and 23.

[83] *Land and Environment Court Act 1979* (NSW).

[84] R Lyster, Z Lipman, N Franklin, G Wiffen & L Pearson, *Environmental and Planning Law in New South Wales*, The Federation Press, Sydney, 2007.

[85] See for example J Holder, *Environmental Assessment: The Regulation of Decision Making*, Oxford University Press, Oxford, 2004.

[86] For example State of Victoria, *Native Vegetation Management: A Framework for Action,* 2002.

[87] G Smith, *Deliberative Democracy and the Environment*, Routledge, New York and London, 2003.

[88] *Environment Protection and Biodiversity Conservation Act 1999* (Cth), s 487.

[89] Australian Network of Environmental Defender's Offices, *Submission to the Independent Review of the Environment Protection and Biodiversity Conservation Act 1999,* January 2009, particularly p. 88 onwards.

[90] Such as occurred in *Blue Wedges Inc v Minister for the Environment, Heritage and the Arts (No 2)* [2008] FCA 1106 (Unreported, North J, 15 July 2008).

[91] Schlosberg, 2007, loc. cit. The view that recognition be attached to ecosystems rather than individual species is not universally shared, notably among animal ethicists. This is acknowledged by Schlosberg.

[92] Bosselmann, loc.cit.

[93] See for example section 4A of the *Water Act 1989* (Vic), which defines the 'Environmental Water Reserve'. Other sections of the Act permit the Minister to allocate a water entitlement to maintain the Reserve (s 48B), or to reject an application for water entitlement that might threaten the Reserve (s 55). See also the *Australian International Agreement on a National Water Initiative 2004,* Viewed on 30 October 2009, <http://www.nwc.gov.au/nwi/index.cfm>, which conflates environmental flows with flows for 'public benefit'.

[94] 16 USC 1531-1544.

[95] In the Channel Deepening Project two environmental impact assessments did not investigate the effects of dredging on non-endangered and non-commercial fisheries. See: Victorian National Parks Association, *Submission on the Supplementary Environment Effects Statement of The Proposed Channel Deepening Project in Port Phillip Bay,* May 2007, Viewed on 30 October 2009, <http://www.vnpa.org.au/subsection.php?subsection_id=43>.

[96] Sections 114 and 119 of the *Planning and Environment Act 1987* (Vic).

[97] Currently section 219 of the *Protection of the Environment Operations Act 1997* (NSW) prevents the Land and Environment Court from granting leave to bring enforcement or prosecution proceedings if the government's environmental agency decides to take another, potentially less severe, action to address the alleged offence.

[98] Government funding for community legal representation would obviate the need for community groups to seek protective costs orders, which like the civil enforcement case of *Blue Mountains Conservation Society Inc v Delta Electricity* [2009] NSWLEC 150 (Unreported, Pain J, 9 September 2009) are liable to be appealed thus delaying the delivery of justice.

[99] Schlosberg, 2007, loc. cit.

Bibliography

Adams, W., *Green Development: Environment and Sustainability in the Third World*. Routledge, London, 2001 (2nd ed).

Agyeman, J., Bullard, R. & Evans, B., (eds), *Just Sustainabilities: Development in an Unequal World*. The MIT Press, Cambridge Massachusetts, 2003.

Agyeman, J., *Sustainable Communities and the Challenge of Environmental Justice*. New York University Press, New York, 2005.

Australian Network of Environmental Defender's Offices, *Submission to the Independent Review of the Environment Protection and Biodiversity Conservation Act 1999*. January, 2009.

Barry, B, 'Sustainable and Intergenerational Justice'. Dobson, A. (ed), *Fairness and Futurity: Essays on Environmental Sustainability and Social Justice*. Oxford University Press, Oxford, 1999.

Beever, A., 'Aristotle on Equity, Law and Justice'. *Legal Theory*. Vol. 10, No. 1, 2004, pp. 33-50.

Biscoe, P. (Justice), *Ecologically Sustainable Development in New South Wales*. Paper delivered on 2 June 2007 at the 5th Worldwide Colloquium of the IUCN Academy of Environmental Law. Paraty, Brazil.

Bosselman, B.,'Ecological Justice and Law'. *Environmental Law for Sustainability*. Richardson, B. & Wood, S. (eds). Hart Publishing, Oxford and Portland, Oregon, 2006.

Brunnée, J., 'Climate Change, Global Environmental Justice and International Environmental Law'. *Environmental Law and Justice in Context*. Ebbesson, J. & Okowa, P. (eds), Cambridge University Press, Cambridge, 2009.

Callewaert, J., 'The Multiple and Competing Conceptions of Environmental Justice'. *Global Citizenship and Environmental Justice*. Shallcros, T. & Robinson, J. (eds), Rodopi, Amsterdam, 2006.

Charlesworth, H., 'The High Court and Human Rights'. *Centenary Essays for the High Court of Australia*. LexisNexis Butterworths, Sydney, 2004, pp. 356-369.

Commonwealth of Australia, *National Strategy for Ecologically Sustainable Development*. 1992.

Dobson, A., *Justice and the Environment: Conceptions of Environmental Sustainability and Dimensions of Social Justice*. Oxford University Press, Oxford, 1998.

Eckersley, R., *Environmentalism and Political Theory: Towards an Ecocentric Approach*. UCL Press, London, 1992.

Fleisher-Trainor, S., 'Realms of Value: Conflicting Natural Resource Values and Incommensurability'. *Environmental Values*. Vol. 15 No. 1, pp. 3-27.

Gerrard, M. & Foster, S. (eds), *The Law of Environmental Justice: Theories and Procedures to Address Disproportionate Risks*. American Bar Association, Chicago, 2008 (2nd ed).

Harvey, D., 'The Environment of Justice'. *Living With Nature: Environmental Politics as Cultural Discourse*. Fischer, F. & Hajer, M. (eds). Oxford University Press, Oxford, 1999, chapter 8.

Hajer, M., *The Politics of Environmental Discourse: Ecological Modernization and the Policy Process*. Oxford University Press, Oxford, 1995.

Hoban, R. & Brooks, T., *Green Justice: The Environment and the Courts*. Westview Press, Boulder, 1996 (2nd ed).

Holder, J., *Environmental Assessment: The Regulation of Decision Making*. Oxford University Press, Oxford, 2004.

International Union for Conservation of Nature and Natural Resources, *The IUCN Red List of Threatened Species*. 2009, data version 2009, Viewed on 1 August 2009, <http://www.iucnredlist.org>.

Lee, M., *EU Environmental Law: Challenges, Change and Decision-Making*. Hart Publishing, Oxford and Portland, Oregon, 2005.

Low, N. & Gleeson B., *Justice, Society and Nature: An Exploration of Political Ecology*. Routledge, London, 1998.

Lyster, R., Lipman, Z., Franklin, N., Wiffen, G. & Pearson, L., *Environmental and Planning Law in New South Wales*. The Federation Press, Sydney, 2007.

Mason, M., *Environmental Democracy*. Earthscan, London, 1999.

Meadowcroft, J., 'Participation and Sustainable Development: Modes of Citizen, Community and Organisational Involvement'. *Governance for Sustainable Development: The Challenge of Adapting Form to Function*. Edgar Elgar Press, Cheltenham, 2004.

Midley, M., 'Duties Concerning Island States'. *Environmental Philosophy*. University of Queensland Press, St Lucia, 1983.

Radcliffe, J., *Green Politics: Dictatorship or Democracy?* Palgrave, Basingstoke, Hampshire and New York, 2002.

Rechtschaffen, C. & Gauna, E. (eds), *Environmental Justice: Law, Policy and Regulation*. Carolina Academic Press, Durham, North Carolina, 2003 (2nd ed).

Rowe, G., 'Environmental Justice as an Ethical, Economic and Legal Principle'. *Environmental Justice and Market Mechanisms: Key Challenges for Environmental Law and Policy*. Kluwer Law International, London, 1999.

Sabatier, P., 'Knowledge, Policy Orientated Learning and Policy Change: An Advocacy Coalition Framework'. *Knowledge: Creation, Diffusion, Utilization*. Vol. 8, 1987, p 649.

Schlosberg, D., *Defining Environmental Justice: Theories, Movements, and Nature*. Oxford University Press, Oxford, 2007.

Schlosberg, D., 'Reconceiving Environmental Justice: Global Movements and Political Theories'. *Environmental Politics*. Vol. 13, No. 3, 2004, pp. 517-540.

Schlosberg, D., *Environmental Justice and the New Pluralism*. Oxford University Press, Oxford, 1999.

Sen, A., *Development as Freedom*. Oxford University Press, Oxford, 1999.

Shelton, D., 'Environmental Justice in the Postmodern World'. *Environmental Justice and Market Mechanisms: Key Challenges for Environmental Law and Policy*. Kluwer Law International, London, 1999.

Shrader-Frechette, K., *Environmental Justice: Creating Equality, Reclaiming Democracy*. Oxford University Press, New York, 2002.

Smith, G., *Deliberative Democracy and the Environment*. Routledge, New York and London, 2003.

Stone, C., 'Should Trees have Standing? Toward Legal Rights for Natural Objects'. *Should Trees have Standing? And Other Essays on Law, Morals and the Environment*. Oxford University Press, Oxford, 1996, (25th anniversary ed).

Victorian National Parks Association, *Submission on the Supplementary Environment Effects Statement of The Proposed Channel Deepening Project in Port Phillip Bay*. May 2007, Viewed on 30 October 2009, <http://www.vnpa.org.au/subsection.php?subsection_id=43>.

Woolf, H., *The Pursuit of Justice*. Oxford University Press, Oxford.

Brad Jessup is a Teaching Fellow with the ANU College of Law at The Australian National University. Brad teaches environmental law subjects to law and non-law students and researches across environmental disciplines. Brad is currently researching concepts of environmental justice.

Teaching Environmental Law in the 21st Century

Erika Techera

Abstract

Environmental law emerged as a university subject in the 1990s but has evolved far beyond its origins. As the range and complexity of environmental laws has expanded so too has the job of teaching environmental law. However, this is not simply a matter of enlarging the number of subjects or substantive laws that are taught. It is clear that the field of environmental regulation has evolved from a series of media-specific statutes to much more integrated regimes. These complexities and the increasing interconnectedness of legal issues with other areas of environmental studies necessitate students developing an understanding of the role of law as well as other disciplines. Environmental legal education must engage with, involve an appreciation of and embrace inter-disciplinarity and multi-skilling. Environmental law, perhaps more than any other legal field, cannot be taught in a vacuum. This chapter will address the changing manner in which environmental law is taught. It will consider ways in which environmental law teachers can incorporate interdisciplinary perspectives and comparative studies into the classroom to facilitate the development of the necessary skills and knowledge in law students to meet future challenges.

Key Words: Environmental law, environmental education, inter-disciplinarity, legal education, sustainability, tertiary sector teaching.

*****

1.   Introduction

Good environmental governance is essential if current issues such as biodiversity loss and ecosystem degradation are to be addressed. Legal regulation plays a significant part in any environmental governance regime and therefore environmental law is an important component for achieving good environmental governance. The law is an important tool to regulate and protect the environment, but also change human behaviour in relation to nature. It is clear that in teaching students both aspects of the role of law must therefore be explained.

Environmental law emerged as a university subject area in the 1990s but has evolved far beyond its origins in local government planning law.[1] The diversity and complexity of environmental law has already been noted by Jessup in this volume.[2] At its broadest it covers topics such as planning and land use management, biodiversity and wildlife protection, natural and cultural heritage conservation, natural resource management, water and marine regulation, pollution and climate change. In addition it involves a consideration of legal rights and remedies in areas such as administrative and constitutional law, tort, contract and crime.

While environmental law is a field which is expanding rapidly in terms of its content, it is also gaining in popularity as the extent of environmental degradation becomes more widely known and broad - governmental and non-governmental, corporate and public - participation in solutions is encouraged.

However, environmental law is not a core or compulsory subject in most undergraduate and graduate law (LLB) curricula.[3] For a long time there was even some question as to whether environmental law was a separate subject area suitable for the university programme.[4] Indeed still today, there is a tendency by some to suggest that legal practitioners in this field are not 'real lawyers'. This is enlightening because one of the reasons it may not be considered a 'proper legal subject' is that it draws upon and incorporates a range of non-law disciplines. Jessup, in his chapter in this volume, confirms the importance of inter-disciplinarity to environmental law.[5] In the past law courses focused heavily upon purely legal concepts and black letter law. However, it is clear that environmental law is informed by other legal areas such as human rights,[6] jurisprudence, ethics and legal philosophy.[7] Many other disciplines are also relevant including the physical and social sciences, environmental studies, politics and international relations. It is clear that graduates of environmental law programmes, whether practising lawyers or not, will need to develop an understanding of the role of other disciplines in addressing environmental issues in order to contribute positively to this growing field.

The purpose of this chapter is to consider the changing context in which environmental law is taught and what separates it from other areas of the legal curriculum. Thereafter, the aim is to explore what this means for teachers of environmental law and to offer some suggestions on curricula and methodologies. In large part this chapter draws upon the personal experiences of the author teaching domestic and international law and non-law students, in Australia, enrolled in environmental law undergraduate and postgraduate programmes.[8]

The first section of this chapter will consider in detail the context in which environmental law is taught in terms of the University setting, student cohort and rapidly expanding subject area. This will be followed by a consideration of why the teaching of environmental law needs to change and ways and means by which this might be achieved. Finally, conclusions will be drawn as to the future of environmental legal education.

2.   The Context of Contemporary Environmental Law Teaching

The University setting is changing in a number of ways which impact upon the teaching of environmental law and many other subjects. However, for teachers of environmental law these changes are compounded by a transforming student cohort and rapidly expanding subject area. These three very relevant contexts are considered below as they inform the development of environmental legal education curricula.

A. The Changing University Environment

The tertiary sector is becoming much more business-oriented.[9] In the past universities were run in a public service-like style but more recently a corporate type model has been adopted. For example, this can be illustrated by the increasing focus upon the economic viability of degree programmes. This new focus has also translated into students being seen as 'customers' whose needs must be satisfied. Therefore, in designing curricular academics must take much greater account of student expectations of the university experience. This will be considered further below in the context of the student cohort.

A second incidence of this shifting attitude is that a more centralised approach has been taken by universities in the development of curricula. This can be seen from the flurry of curriculum reviews and learning and teaching plans resulting in the setting of graduate attributes or capabilities to be embedded as core values in students university-wide.[10] In many cases these attributes include inter-disciplinarity, sustainability, internationalisation and global citizenship which are key themes of this conference.[11] At Macquarie University in Sydney 'core values of Scholarship, Ethical Practice, Sustainability and Engagement are seen as the Guiding Principles within which the curriculum is developed'.[12] These more centralised approaches have been criticised by some as causing tensions between university management and departments.[13] Nonetheless, their development directly affects the ways in which curricula are designed and teaching is undertaken.

A third aspect of the changing university sector is what Bridges refers to as the removal of 'boundaries' that once existed in universities, classifying the changes as spatial (both the physical university environs and 'virtual' spaces), temporal (the changing university academic day, week and year) and social (evolving scholarly and student communities).[14] He predicts that these trends will continue into the 21st century and contrasts this modern experience with a 'traditional university setting' in which students learnt in a narrow physical environment, in a 'tightly defined academic community' during a 'concentrated academic year'.[15]

B. The Diversifying Student Cohort

The range of students enrolled in environmental law courses is perhaps the most diverse of all areas of law[16] in terms of both their nationalities and educational backgrounds. Firstly, students may be international or domestic, come from many different cultures and with different personal histories and have a wide range of nationalities. This brings considerable strengths to the classroom in terms of the perspectives and cultural viewpoints which may be shared. However, it also presents some challenges, predominantly in terms of language but also related to the differences in culture and legal tradition in the countries from which students originate.

The second area of diversity is the range of experience and expertise of the student cohort. In the past environmental law subjects, within law schools, tended to include only law students. However, this is no longer the case.[17] Particularly in Masters programmes students are drawn from a range of educational backgrounds, occupations and with a variety of qualifications. They may include, for example, planners, environmental consultants, conservation biologists, hydrologists, environmental engineers, policymakers, politics, lawyers and other physical and social sciences. Whilst these postgraduate students are likely to be mature, highly motivated and in many cases experts in their own fields, they usually have little experience of the law.

It is important to identify and appreciate these backgrounds as they are relevant to and inform student expectations. Where students are drawn from environmentally-related professions they are often studying environmental law with the specific goal of filling a gap in their knowledge - in order to understand how to 'think like a lawyer' or at least to 'understand how lawyers think'. In many cases they wish to apply their studies in their workplace as they may be required to provide a link between their industry and the legal profession. For example, students may be team leaders who work with in-house counsel or have the responsibility for making the decision to engage solicitors or barristers to provide legal advice. In other cases these graduates could be future members of statutory advisory panels or law- and policy-makers on Government boards or with international environmental agencies. Of course some students may have no environmental or legal experience or educational background, and therefore this must also be recognised and addressed in curriculum design and teaching.

The last observation relates to the prior knowledge of the law these students may have. In some cases they may have quite detailed knowledge of the law in the specific area in which they work. For example, planners tend to know a great deal about town planning legislation and development assessment procedures and regulations. Another example is conservation biologists who are adept at quoting sections of statutes such as the threatened species legislation. This prior awareness can be a strength but also a weakness if students find it difficult to overcome ingrained perceptions of the law and legal process.

To add to this complexity environmental law is often being taught to both law and non-law students together. For example, at Macquarie University in Sydney the legally qualified Master of Laws (LLM) students are taught together with those enrolled in the non-law environmental Masters programmes. Furthermore, in some cases Bachelor of Laws undergraduate units are cross-accredited in other degree programmes such as a Bachelor of Planning. Therefore, as well as the qualifications and experience of the students being diverse, their expectations of learning outcomes in any given environmental law class can also vary widely depending upon the programme the students are enrolled in and the stage they are at in their studies.

C. The Expanding Range of Environmental Laws

Environmental law is a rapidly evolving field. For example, in the international context, there has been a well-documented exponential growth in multilateral environmental agreements (MEAs) over the last few decades.[18] In addition to this there is a growing body of regional and bilateral agreements as well as domestic law. These laws do not exist in isolation and are vertically (such as international law which must be implemented nationally and also locally) and horizontally (in terms of intersecting areas such as biodiversity conservation, land use planning and pollution control, for example) connected, affecting both their implementation and enforcement.

National law has also progressed well beyond town planning law and pollution control statutes which once dominated this area.[19] Today the body of environmental law includes these areas but many others such as water law, marine protection, biodiversity conservation, climate change law and heritage conservation and policy.[20] In addition there are a number of cross-cutting areas such as corporate social responsibility, trade and environment, human rights and the right to a healthy environment, and Indigenous peoples and the management of their natural resources. These add to the range and complexity of environmental laws which in turn increases the difficulty of teaching this subject area.[21]

Gone are the days when there was some concern as to whether environmental law truly was an appropriate area of law to be studied within a law course. It is now firmly established as a subject of law albeit often one covering different content depending upon the university in which it is being taught. As environmental law is of critical importance in achieving good environmental governance, it is a significant subject area for those undertaking legal studies.

3.   Teaching Environmental Law in the Contemporary Context

The question for legal academics charged with the task of teaching environmental law is how to address the issues identified in the above contextual analysis. Clearly environmental law is here to stay with growing popularity not only amongst professionals but also the general populace. Where once environmental law was offered to students on an irregular basis with low enrolments, now it is a fashionable subject area attracting an ever increasing cohort of students.

But this increased attention comes at a time of great change. With the growth in the subject area come challenges: the need to cover a great deal of subject material and develop key student skills in a changing university setting. At the same time demands are also being placed upon academics in two other key areas: First, teaching practices are being affected by centralised management and the expertise of the contemporary tertiary teacher is changing with an increasing academic focus upon the scholarship of teaching and learning.[22] Secondly, academics are being asked to take on greater administrative roles whilst also increasing their research output.

The challenge is for legal academics to deal with this teaching conundrum under considerable pressure. Rather than seeing this as a problematic burden, it could also be viewed as a challenge and opportunity for diversification of teaching practices. Now is the time to change the way that environmental law is taught in order to meet this challenge and to rethink teaching practices in light of the combination of new skills and substantive knowledge needed by graduates. These issues will be explored in the next section.

4.   Curricula and Methodologies

There is a large body of literature related to quality teaching and student learning in the tertiary sector, both generally and related specifically to legal education.[23] This literature cannot be considered in detail here. Rather the purpose is to draw attention to key trends that necessarily impact upon any discussion of the teaching of environmental law.

First, there is a trend towards outcomes-based education and student-centred rather than teacher-focused learning.[24] This is important because it is impacted upon by student expectations which ultimately require an understanding of the student cohort.

Secondly, there is an increasing focus in education literature upon constructive alignment.[25] It is well recognised that learning activities and assessments must be constructively aligned with learning outcomes. These learning outcomes need to be informed not only by good teaching practices but by student expectations. Equally students must be engaged in learning activities in order to achieve the learning outcomes.

Thirdly, there is a turn away from traditional lecture and tutorial modes of teaching to a wider variety of class structures and activities including workshops and seminars not constrained by the physical classroom.[26] In part this is a reflection of the technology now available which permits classes to be taught in virtual environments as well as the utilisation of whole of environment software and social networking tools such as online chat rooms, discussion boards and blogs.

However, these developments do not address the specific subject areas that must be taught. In the context of legal education there is a need to overcome the traditional segregated approach which has focused upon law being taught isolation from other subject areas. Despite the fact that in most cases undergraduate students are studying law as part of a double degree (or graduate) programme, and postgraduate students invariably have qualifications in another discipline, law is still taught in a 'siloed' fashion. In most cases interconnectedness between subject areas is limited to linkages between environmental law and other legal areas such as contract, tort and administrative law. But this ill equips graduates to deal with the multi- and inter-disciplinary contexts in which they are likely to work. There is concern that teaching in this area 'has not provided students sufficient understanding of the complex systems that form the bulk of environmental law'.[27] Lawyers practising in the environmental law field will need to be able to understand and work with people from many other disciplines. For example, those involved in environmental litigation will need to be able to explore complex issues with expert witnesses drawn from many fields such as planning, environmental science, conservation biology, hydrology and increasingly atmospheric science in the context of climate change. Non-lawyers are likely to be required to establish linkages between their own disciplines and environmental law - to form a bridge between one or many areas of environmental study.

As noted above the subject matter now comprised within the field of environmental law is huge. But it is not enough simply to expand the range of topic areas covered. Changes are needed in the way environmental law is taught to incorporate much broader substantive material drawn from multi- and inter-disciplinary fields. To illustrate, one of the focuses of this volume is environmental ethics. It is critical that students studying environmental law also develop an understanding of this area. In order to embed ethics in legislation, as suggested by Jessup in this volume, it is essential that students understand the philosophies that underpin environmental thinking.

Therefore, environmental law subjects must include broader substantive material but they must also facilitate the development of graduate skills - both generic and specific skills that they will need in the workplace.[28] Studying environmental law is not just about learning statutes and cases. The identification of innovative approaches and design of new environmental laws is clearly important in addressing future challenges.[29] In order to identify new legal tools and draft effective environmental laws graduates must, for example, develop problem solving and critical thinking skills. The foundation for these skills must be taught at university alongside substantive legal material.

Environmental law is different from other more traditional subjects taught in law schools as many graduates will not practise law. In order to ensure that these students can meet future challenges in the area of environmental governance and sustainability, there must be an increased focus on inter-disciplinarity and green skilling in environmental law curricula.

Whilst a legal education curriculum should not be designed purely around the needs of industry, nor be solely student-centred, it is clear that increasingly there is pressure being placed on universities to develop graduate capabilities in students that are required by industry.[30] Contemporaneously, literature on education draws attention to the need to identify methods which 'encourage a transition from dependence in learning to independence'.[31] This call to change teaching practices is reflected to a certain extent in the literature on legal education. There has been a turn away from teaching law via case studies and legislative analyses alone.[32] Whilst it is recognised that these remain important they do not address the inherent inter-disciplinarity in environmental law nor the diversity of the student cohort. Furthermore, the literature on best practice education more generally refers to the development of learning activities viewed through the student lens and with an inherent student-centred focus. Therefore, perhaps the greatest changes are needed in the methodologies of teaching environmental law, in order to incorporate the knowledge and skills referred to above.

5.   Contemporary Teaching of Environmental Law

Having identified the need to change teaching practices it is necessary to consider how this can be achieved. Two key areas are identified here: Firstly, in order to identify more diversified learning activities and teaching methodologies, lessons can be learnt from other disciplines. These can be drawn upon to develop learning activities not traditionally used in legal education. Secondly, the expertise of students in the classroom can be harnessed and utilised to great effect.

A. Borrowing Ideas from Other Disciplines

Problem based learning (PBL) is one possible model for achieving multiple outcomes in the context of a mixed cohort and inter-disciplinary subject area. PBL involves facilitating student learning through the exploration of a structured research problem in small self-directed groups with the tutor acting as facilitator.[33] A key characteristic of PBL is that it shifts responsibility for learning onto the student,[34] and takes a constructivist approach to learning and teaching[35] in which students learn how to learn.[36] PBL is thus a 'learning method more than a teaching method'.[37]

PBL was pioneered in medical education[38] and the teaching of clinical sciences[39] but has spread to many other disciplines[40] such as psychology.[41] Whilst it has been used widely in medical schools, true PBL is less common in legal education and has rarely completely replaced the lecture-tutorial model. More commonly problem-solving, rather than true PBL, is used. Whilst problem-solving maybe 'the most important skill a lawyer can acquire',[42] it is only one of the objectives of PBL methodology. Problem solving in this context involves a practically oriented 'problem' which can be answered by the use of materials provided - such as the textbook and lecture notes. PBL is much broader involving the answering of a problem that the student has never seen before and which requires research, reading and analysis beyond what has been provided.[43] PBL involves students working through a model involving identification of the problem, issues and goals, research, analysis, peer sharing, discussion, development of solutions, reflection and debriefing.[44] Students must acquire substantive knowledge and develop skills in the course of exploring solutions to the problem.

Where PBL has been used in legal education it has predominantly been in the context of practical legal training.[45] This is completed after a Bachelor degree and is the final step prior to obtaining a practising certificate to work as a lawyer. Such courses are of short duration (around 3-6 months) and are by their very nature practical programmes. But arguably PBL lends itself more broadly to legal education primarily because law involves problem solving in circumstances where there is rarely a right and wrong answer and so learning how to learn, freely and fully, is particularly beneficial.[46] Furthermore, environmental law, in particular, involves inter-disciplinary study which is ideally suited to the PBL method.

Depending upon the design of the problem, PBL can build skills so that students can better apply themselves in the workplace - be that in legal practise or a non-legal environment. The 'problems' must be broadened well beyond the traditional case simulations[47] and client-practitioner role plays.[48] Other contexts could be included which would be relevant to a broader cohort of students. For example, a role play, such as a facilitated negotiation, could be used which incorporates legal as well as non-law roles centred on a legal issue.

Other examples include students drafting a briefing note on a new law for their workplace team; identifying legislative 'gaps' and drafting submissions on law reform; corporate briefings; and delivering community-based workshop training. It is possible that further diversity could also be included, for example, a truly inter-disciplinary problem could be devised that involves both the application of scientific data and analysis of legal issues.[49]

Furthermore, other learning activities can be developed based upon teaching and learning practices used in other discipline areas. Students could be asked to negotiate a new protocol to a treaty in the context of a model United Nations conference where students represent states, NGOs and UN agencies.[50] Alternatively students could be asked to re-negotiate an Indigenous co-management agreement for a National Park. These are the equivalent of the design studios utilised in the teaching of architecture. Students are asked to workshop ideas in groups and identify creative solutions to more complex, larger tasks. Again this is supported by the literature in relation to PBL.

An example of another type of learning activity, underutilised in legal education, is field studies. In many other disciplines field trips are used quite extensively. Whilst in law a field trip might be arranged to see a court, their utilisation is generally limited. However, this activity could be used to great effect to link environmental issues with the implementation of environmental law. For example, planning law students could visit a municipal council and walk around a suburb identifying aspects of a local environment plan 'in action', observe by-laws in place and conservation orders in operation. Similarly clinical programmes also provide particularly useful experiential learning opportunities.[51] Again PBL can provide a strong foundation for such internships and placements.

Although the planning and development of these learning activities maybe resource intensive, by designing suitable activities significant content can be included along with skill-building thus achieving multiple outcomes. There may well be a much greater role for web- and computer-based learning in this context. Thus whilst planning and design may be resource intensive time savings could be made in terms of delivery.[52] It is clear that web- and computer-based learning is under-utilised in legal education and this has been the subject of comment for some time.[53] In many cases eLearning is limited to the use of electronic databases or 'whole of environment' solutions which assist in delivery – such as web-based access to iLectures, course materials and discussion forums. One possibility here is that 'live' practice clinics could be held online or virtual worlds, such as Second Life, utilised for mock trials. This is directly relevant to the practice of law where many courts now have telephone and online conference facilities. It also builds important skills relevant to other fields such as government-based work in rural and remote areas. Beyond mere delivery, research has been undertaken in relation to the use of artificial intelligence in legal education.[54] In particular, Aleven's investigation of systems which incorporate legal arguments that barristers make in court suggests that web- and computer-based learning may have a much greater role to play in developing legal reasoning and other such skills in the future.

B. Use of In-Class Expertise

Classes in environmental law attract a diverse cohort of students, as noted above. These students bring invaluable knowledge, expertise and qualifications to the classroom. This is often seen as a negative in terms of the challenges posed in bringing these students 'up to speed' in relation to the law. But it also provides an excellent opportunity to share knowledge and expertise. This empowers and engages students and also assists in understanding the complexity of issues and the different perspectives from which environmental law issues can be seen. The expertise of these students in the class can be utilised to teach the importance of environmental law in a multi-disciplinary context. Multi-stakeholder role plays can be constructed which provide an opportunity to understand the intricacy of environmental issues and the perspectives of various actors. For example, negotiation exercises can be developed around a development consent and land use planning issue. Students can initially be asked to take on roles aligned with their own areas of expertise or experience: such as government officers, local council planner, Indigenous community member, environmental activist, commercial developer, conservation consultant or local resident. A reverse role play can then give students the opportunity to play an unfamiliar part in which they are forced to consider another perspective and learn substantive material associated with that role. Such a role play could involve detailed consideration of case law and legislation. But it could also incorporate inter-disciplinary perspectives and issues such as environmental justice, Indigenous peoples rights, environmental ethics, scientific evidence and local politics.

Whilst student expertise is often used in classroom group discussion, it is clear that there is much greater potential for its utilisation in a broader range of learning activities. Again these learning activities are supported by the education literature in relation to PBL and experiential learning.

6.   Conclusions

What emerges from the above discussion is that courses in environmental law are growing in popularity and attracting a diversifying cohort, but at the same time increasing pressures is being placed upon academics working in the tertiary sector. Whilst academics are used to designing curricula to achieve multiple aims this has been done in a very isolated way in the design of law subjects, both in terms of assessments and also in relation to learning activities. It is apparent from the above consideration of the context of environmental law teaching that more must be done in less time and perhaps also with less physical resources. Whilst virtual environments and web-based learning activities offer some advantages in this context, it is still the case that multiple objectives need to be achieved in face-to-face class time, in relation to both the substantive subject matter and development of key skills. It is in this context that PBL emerges as a model that deserves further attention in relation to contemporary environmental legal education.[55] Exposure to real world problems builds research, reasoning, critical analysis and problem-solving skills along with many other graduate attributes such as a commitment to life-long learning, and the ability to work in a team.

There is little doubt that the incorporation of problem-based and experiential learning, field trips and the teaching of key skills will place a heavy administrative burden on legal academics. However, it is clear that this is necessary for the teaching of environmental law and increasingly being demanded by students and central university management.

There is relatively little literature specifically related to the teaching of environmental law. However, for the reasons noted above further research in this area is warranted and a detailed consideration of this area of legal education is overdue.[56] There is much to be learnt from both other disciplines and the students themselves. Legal education must embrace inter-disciplinarity to allow graduates, whether they are lawyers or non-lawyers, to develop the knowledge and skills to address environmental problems and identify potential solutions.

Notes

[1] UK Centre for Legal Education, *Teaching Environmental Law*, Viewed on 20 January 2009, <http://www.ukcle.ac.uk/research/projects/environmental. html>.

[2] B Jessup, 'Investing the Law with an Environmental Ethic: Using an Environmental Justice Theory for Change', *Environmental Law, Ethics & Governance*, E Techera (ed), Inter-Disciplinary Press, Oxford, 2010.

[3] A quick review of legal programmes from several continents clearly indicates this: For example, Macquarie University, Australia, Viewed 1 August 2009, <http://www.law.mq.edu.au/html/undergraduate/compulsory. htm>; Harvard Law School, USA, Viewed 1 August 2009, <http://www. law.harvard.edu/academics/degrees/jd/pos/index.html>; University College London, UK, Viewed 1 August 2009, <http://www.ucl.ac.uk/laws/ prospective/undergraduate/index.shtml?llb_hons>.

[4] In 1981 the following article was published in which the author makes the case for the teaching of environmental law at university: GJ Cano, 'Education in Environmental Law', *The Environmentalist*, Vol. 1 (4) (1981) pp. 259-266.

[5] ibid.

[6] This is illustrated by Lewis in her chapter in this volume: B Lewis, 'The Role of Human Rights in Environmental Governance: The Challenge of Climate Change', *Environmental Law, Ethics & Governance*, E Techera (ed), Inter-Disciplinary Press, Oxford, 2010.

[7] See for example H Nalukenge, 'Environmental Ethics is Key to Sustainability in a Contemporary Society', *Environmental Law, Ethics & Governance*, E Techera (ed), Inter-Disciplinary Press, Oxford, 2010.

[8] This author teaches in the Centre for Environmental Law at Macquarie University in Sydney. Currently five undergraduate environmental electives units are offered as well as seventeen postgraduate units accredited in multiple programmes. The postgraduate programmes involve domestic and international law and non-law graduates in the same classroom context.

[9] J Biggs & C Tang, *Teaching for Quality Learning at University*, Open University Press, Maidenhead, 3rd Edition, 2007, pp.1-2.

[10] For example, Macquarie University, *Review of Academic Programmes White Paper*, Viewed 1 August 2009, <http://www.mq.edu.au/provost/ reports/docs/FINALWHITEPAPER_revised_17102008.doc>; La Trobe University, *Curriculum Review and Renewal at La Trobe University: White Paper*, Viewed 1 August 2009, <http://www.latrobe.edu.au/teaching/assets/ downloads/curriculum/White_Paper_Ac_Board_approved_version.pdf>.

[11] For example, Macquarie University, *Review of Academic Programmes White Paper*, op.cit., p.6.

[12] Ibid.

[13] D Bridges, 'Back to the Future: The Higher Education Curriculum in the 21st Century', *Cambridge Journal of Education,* Vol. 30 (1), 2000, pp. 31-55.

[14] .ibid.

[15] ibid, p.40.

[16] Business law academics might disagree here. However, whilst business law courses do attract many international students from non-law disciplines, they tend to be from the commercial field only. Environmental law attracts students from various fields ranging from the physical to the social sciences, and from politics to linguistics.

[17] This was noted in UKCLE Report, op.cit.

[18] There are over 500 global environmental instruments related to environmental protection: D Craig & MI Jeffery, 'Global Environmental Governance and the United Nations in the 21st Century', Paper presented to the *European Union Forum: Strengthening International Environmental Governance*, Sydney Opera House, 24th November 2006. For an excellent summary of the key instruments see UNEP Register of International Treaties and Other Agreements in the Field of the Environment (2005).

[19] HG Robertson, 'Methods for Teaching Environmental Law: Some Thoughts on Providing Access to the Environmental Law System', *Columbia Journal of Environmental Law*, Vol. 23, 1998, pp.237-298.

[20] This is clear from a review of any current textbook on national environmental law. For example, R Lyster, et al., *Environmental Planning Law in New South Wales*, Federation Press, Annandale, 2nd Ed 2009.

[21] This is commented upon in ZB Plater, 'Environmental Law and Three Economies: Navigating a Sprawling Field of Study, Practice and Societal Governance in which Everything is Connected to Everything Else', *Harvard Environmental Law Review*, Vol. 23, 1999, p. 359.

[22] M Prosser, 'The Scholarship of Teaching and Learning: What is it? A Personal View', *International Journal for the Scholarship of Teaching and Learning*, Vol. 2(2), 2008, pp.1-4.

[23] For example, J Biggs & C Tang, loc. cit.

[24] Ibid, pp. 3 and 20.

[25] Biggs & Tang make it clear that the focus of the book is to 'explain the background and lead you through all the stages of implementing constructive alignment': Ibid, p.7

[26] This is commented upon generally in Biggs & Tang, p.104.

[27] Robertson, op.cit., p.239.

[28] The need to learn skills in association with substantive environmental law is considered in detail in Robertson, op.cit., pp.241-242.

[29] For example, Verbitsky in this volume has explored the Antarctic Treaty System (a very successful legal regime) but also addressed the need to identify and implement new law to address the new challenges of ecotourism in that environment: J Verbitsky, 'Antarctica: The Ticking Clock', *Environmental Law, Ethics & Governance*, E Techera (ed), Inter-Disciplinary Press, Oxford, 2010.

[30] S Thomas & S Busby, 'Do Industry Collaborative Projects Enhance Students' Learning?' *Education & Training,* Vol. 45(4), 2003, p.226; RW Sanson-Fisher & MC Lynagh, 'Problem-Based Learning: A Dissemination Success Story?' *Medical Journal of Australia*, Vol. 183(5), 2005, p.258.

[31] Thomas & Busby, op.cit., p.227.

[32] Ibid p.239-240.

[33] M Newman, *Higher Education Academy Imaginative Curriculum Guide: Problem-Based Learning,* 2004, Viewed 14 November 2009 <http://www. palatine.ac.uk/files/1010.pdf>; YL Wong, 'Harnessing the Potential of Problem-based Learning in Legal Education', *Legal Education Digest*, Vol. 12(3), 2004, pp.21-24.

[34] AB Szabo, 'Teaching Substantive Law through Problem Based Learning in Hong Kong', *Journal of Professional Legal Education*, Vol. 11(2), 1993, pp.195-210.

[35] E Driessen & C Van Der Vleuten, 'Matching Student Assessment to Problem-Based Learning: Lessons from Experience in a Law Faculty', *Studies in Continuing Education*, Vol. 22(2), 2000, pp.235-248.

[36] Szabo, op.cit., p.195.

[37] DA Cruikshank, 'Problem-Based Learning in Legal Education', *Teaching Lawyers' Skills*, J. Webb & C. Maughan (eds), Butterworths, London, 1996, p.188; Szabo, op.cit., p.196.

[38] MC Gwee, 'Globalisation of Problem-Based Learning (PBL): Cross-Cultural Implications', *Kaohsiung Journal of Medical Science*, Vol. 24(3), no.3 Suppl., 2008.

[39] Sanson-Fisher & Lynagh, loc. cit.

[40] W Hung, 'The 9-Step Problem Design Process for Problem-Based Learning: Application of the 3C3R Model', *Educational Research Review*, Vol. 4, 2009, pp.118-141.

[41] SE Severiens & HG Schmidt, 'Academic and Social Integration and Study Progress in Problem-Based Learning', *Higher Education*, Vol. 58, 2009, pp.59-69.

[42] S Nathanson, 'Creating Problems for Law Students: The Key to Teaching Legal Problem Solving', *Journal of Professional Legal Education*, Vol. 10(1), 1992, pp. 1-21, p.1.

[43] Szabo, loc. cit; Hung, loc. cit.

[44] Wong, loc. cit.

[45] J MacKinnon, 'Problem-Based Learning and New Zealand Legal Education', *Web Journal of Current Legal Issues* 2006, Viewed 12 November 2009 <http://webjcli.ncl.ac.uk/2006/issue3/mackinnon3.html>; Szabo, loc. cit.; K Winsor, 'Applying Problem-Based Learning to Practical Legal Training', *The Challenge of Problem-Based Learning*, D Boud & G Feletti (eds), Kogan, London, 2007, (2nd Ed).

[46] Szabo, op.cit., p.195.

[47] Robinson-Dorn, op.cit., p.638.

[48] Robertson, op.cit. p.264.

[49] DA Cancilla, 'Integration of Environmental Analytical Chemistry with Environmental Law: The Development of a Problem-Based Laboratory', *Journal of Chemical Education*, Vol. 78(12), 2001, pp.1652-1660.

[50] Many universities run versions of the Model United Nations workshops. For example, American Model United Nations, Viewed on 3 August 2009 <http://www.amun.org/>; Asia Pacific Model United Nations, Viewed on 3 August 2009, <http://www.amunc.net>.

[51] M Robinson-Dorn, 'Teaching Environmental Law in the Era of Climate Change: A Few What's, Why's and How's', *Washington Law Review*, Vol. 82 (2007) pp.619-648, p.639; Robertson, op.cit., pp.266-270.

[52] J Kellett, *Improving Balance and Mobility through Problem-Based Learning*. Paper presented at ASCILITE Conference, Brisbane 2005.

[53] For example, A Paliwala, 'Transforming Legal Learning', *Computers Education*, Vol. 19(1/2), 1992, pp.113-124.

[54] V Aleven, 'Using Background Knowledge in Case-Based Legal Reasoning: A Computational Model and an Intelligent Learning Environment', *Artificial Intelligence*, Vol. 150, 2003, pp.183-237.

[55] Cruikshank, loc. cit; MacKinnon, loc. cit.

[56] A recent subject survey was conducted by the UK Centre for Legal Education. The survey aims included identifying what is being taught under the banner of Environmental Law'; to whom and by whom such courses were being taught; and how the courses are being taught including the factors which influence teaching and learning strategies: UKCLE, *Teaching Environmental Law*, op.cit.

Bibliography

Aleven, V., 'Using Background Knowledge in Case-Based Legal Reasoning: A Computational Model and an Intelligent Learning Environment'. *Artificial Intelligence*. Vol. 150, 2003, pp. 183-237.

American Model United Nations. Viewed on 3 August 2009 <http://www.amun.org/>.

Asia Pacific Model United Nations. Viewed on 3 August 2009 <http://www.amunc.net>.

Biggs, J. & Tang, C., *Teaching for Quality Learning at University*. 3ʳᵈ Edition, Open University Press, Maidenhead, 2007.

Bridges, D., 'Back to the Future: The Higher Education Curriculum in the 21ˢᵗ Century'. *Cambridge Journal of Education*. Vol. 30 (1), 2000, pp. 31-55.

Cancilla, D.A., 'Integration of Environmental Analytical Chemistry with Environmental Law: The Development of a Problem-Based Laboratory'. *Journal of Chemical Education*. Vol. 78(12), 2001, pp. 1652-1660.

Cano, G.J., 'Education in Environmental Law.' *The Environmentalist.* Vol. 1 (4), 1981, pp. 259-266.

Craig, D. & Jeffery, M.I., 'Global Environmental Governance and the United Nations in the 21st Century'. Paper presented to the *European Union Forum: Strengthening International Environmental Governance.* Sydney Opera House, 24th November 2006.

Cruikshank, D.A., 'Problem-Based Learning in Legal Education'. *Teaching Lawyers' Skills.* Webb, J. & Maughan, C. (eds), Butterworths, London, 1996.

Driessen, E. & Van Der Vleuten, C., 'Matching Student Assessment to Problem-Based Learning: Lessons from Experience in a Law Faculty'. *Studies in Continuing Education.* Vol. 22(2), 2000, pp. 235-248.

Gwee, M.C., 'Globalisation of Problem-Based Learning (PBL): Cross-Cultural Implications'. *Kaohsiung Journal of Medical Science.* Vol. 24(3), No. 3 Suppl., 2008.

Harvard Law School, USA, Viewed 1 August 2009, <http://www.law.har vard.edu/academics/degrees/jd/pos/index.html>.

Hung, W., 'The 9-Step Problem Design Process for Problem-Based Learning: Application of the 3C3R Model'. *Educational Research Review.* Vol. 4, 2009, pp. 118-141.

Jessup, B., 'Investing the Law with an Environmental Ethic: Using an Environmental Justice Theory for Change'. *Environmental Law, Ethics & Governance.* Techera, E. (ed.), Inter-Disciplinary Press, Oxford, 2010.

Kellett, J., *Improving Balance and Mobility through Problem-Based Learning.* Paper presented at ASCILITE Conference, Brisbane 2005.

La Trobe University, *Curriculum Review and Renewal at La Trobe University: White Paper.* Viewed 1 August 2009, <http://www.latrobe. edu.au/teaching/assets/downloads/curriculum/White_Paper_Board_ approved _version.pdf>.

Lyster, R., et al., *Environmental Planning Law in New South Wales.* Federation Press, Annandale, 2nd Ed, 2009.

MacKinnon, J., 'Problem-Based Learning and New Zealand Legal Education'. *Web Journal of Current Legal Issues* 2006. Viewed 12 November 2009 <http://webjcli.ncl.ac.uk/2006/issue3/mackinnon3.html>.

Macquarie University, Australia. Viewed 1 August 2009, <http://www. law.mq.edu.au/html/undergraduate/compulsory.htm>.

Macquarie University, *Review of Academic Programmes White Paper*. Viewed 1 August 2009, <http://www.mq.edu.au/provost/reports/docs/ FINALWHITEPAPER_revised_17102008.doc>.

Nathanson, S., 'Creating Problems for Law Students: The Key to Teaching Legal Problem Solving'. *Journal of Professional Legal Education*. Vol. 10(1), 1992, pp. 1-21.

Newman, M., *Higher Education Academy Imaginative Curriculum Guide: Problem-Based Learning*. 2004, Viewed 14 November 2009 <http://www.palatine.ac.uk/files/1010.pdf>.

Paliwala, A., 'Transforming Legal Learning'. *Computers Education*. Vol. 19(1/2), 1992, pp.113-124.

Plater, Z.B., 'Environmental Law and Three Economies: Navigating a Sprawling Field of Study, Practice and Societal Governance in which Everything is Connected to Everything Else'. *Harvard Environmental Law Review*. Vol. 23, 1999, pp. 359-392.

Prosser, M., 'The Scholarship of Teaching and Learning: What is it? A Personal View'. *International Journal for the Scholarship of Teaching and Learning*. Vol. 2(2), 2008, pp.1-4.

Robertson, H.G., 'Methods for Teaching Environmental Law: Some Thoughts on Providing Access to the Environmental Law System'. *Columbia Journal of Environmental Law*. Vol. 23, 1998, pp. 237-298.

Robinson-Dorn, M., 'Teaching Environmental Law in the Era of Climate Change: A Few What's, Why's and How's'. *Washington Law Review*. Vol. 82, 2007, pp. 619-648.

Sanson-Fisher, R.W. & Lynagh, M.C., 'Problem-Based Learning: A Dissemination Success Story?' *Medical Journal of Australia*. Vol. 183(5), 2005, pp. 258-260.

Severiens, S.E. & Schmidt H.G., 'Academic and Social Integration and Study Progress in Problem Based Learning'. *Higher Education*. Vol. 58, 2009, pp. 59-69.

Szabo, A.B., 'Teaching Substantive Law through Problem Based Learning in Hong Kong'. *Journal of Professional Legal Education*. Vol. 11(2), 1993, pp. 195-210.

Thomas, S. & Busby, S., 'Do Industry Collaborative Projects Enhance Students' Learning?' *Education & Training*. Vol. 45(4), 2003, pp. 226-235.

UK Centre for Legal Education, *Teaching Environmental Law*. Viewed on 20 January 2009, <http://www.ukcle.ac.uk/research/projects/environmental.html>.

University College London, UK, Viewed 1 August 2009, <http://www.ucl.ac.uk/laws/prospective/undergraduate/index.shtml?llb_hons>.

Winsor, K., 'Applying Problem-Based Learning to Practical Legal Training'. *The Challenge of Problem-Based Learning*. Boud, D. & Feletti, G. (eds). Kogan, London, 2nd Ed, 2007.

Wong, Y.L., 'Harnessing the Potential of Problem-Based Learning in Legal Education'. *Legal Education Digest*. Vol. 12(3), 2004, pp. 21-24.

Erika Techera, PhD., is a Senior Lecturer at the Centre for International and Environmental Law, School of Law, Macquarie University, Australia. Erika teaches and researches in a range of international and comparative environmental law areas. Her previous experience includes seven years practice as a Barrister in Sydney.

PART II

International Environmental Governance

Antarctica: The Ticking Clock

Jane Verbitsky

Abstract
Although initiated in the heyday of the Cold War, the *Antarctic Treaty* was a triumph of internationalism and multilateralism, establishing common parameters about the status of, objectives for, and activities permitted on, the southernmost continent. The Treaty has survived intact into the post-Cold War era and now forms the critical hub of a system of legal instruments which provide a framework for the governance and management of Antarctica and its immediate environment. The *Antarctic Treaty* has been successful in preventing militarization of the continent, freezing territorial claims, and prioritizing the importance of scientific research as the key activity in Antarctica. However, the system faces challenges relating to tourism and the differing proposed options for the future of Antarctica - common heritage territory, world park, or natural reserve. This chapter explores these intertwined issues and the dilemmas they present for decision-makers against a ticking clock of factors that threaten to overtake the cumbersome ATS decision-making process.

Key Words: Antarctica, tourism, common heritage, world park, natural reserve, governance, sovereignty.

*****

1. Introduction

In the bipolar era of the Cold War the *Antarctic Treaty*[1] was anomalous for what it symbolised: multilateral, international efforts to preserve the non-sovereign status of the world's southernmost continent; prevent militarisation of the territory; promote scientific research in Antarctica; and protect the unique southern polar environment. The collaborative achievements of the *Antarctic Treaty* signatories in these years were at odds with the contemporary arms race between the superpowers and their allies, the armed conflicts in Africa, Asia, and the Americas that erupted over contested territories, and far in advance of the broad recognition of humankind's degradation of the environment and depletion of natural resources. The Treaty parties can congratulate themselves on initiating a regime that has furthered an eco-protectionist agenda, and successfully facilitated consensus amongst a diverse, enlarged group of signatory states about the primacy of peace and scientific endeavours in Antarctica.

In the year of the *Antarctic Treaty's* fiftieth anniversary, though, the Treaty parties face a series of difficult problems concerning firstly, tourism and commercial pressures on Antarctica and its resources and, secondly, decisions concerning the long-term future and status of the continent. These problems arise from different issues and involve both signatory parties and non-parties, but are inter-related. They centre on sovereignty, resource protection, governance, regime compliance, and differing philosophical conceptions of Antarctica's role in the world. These are significant problems. Moreover, the need to resolve them is made more pressing by the rapid rate of global environmental change and the accelerating pace of global warming. Adding to this are the pressures from globalisation that have made Antarctica a more accessible destination, and the technological advances that have enabled vessels more frequently and in greater numbers to voyage to the continent. Effectively, then, the Treaty parties must undertake critical decisions about Antarctica against the background of a ticking clock. The challenge for them will be to make and operationalise those decisions before they are rendered redundant by accident, misadventure, rogue actors, or environmental disaster.

2.   The Antarctic Treaty System

The *Antarctic Treaty* is a relatively short document comprising just fourteen articles. Two overarching themes are outlined in the Preamble to the Treaty: the belief that it is 'in the interests of all mankind that Antarctica shall continue forever to be used exclusively for peaceful purposes and shall not become the scene or object of international discord'; and the conceptualization of international scientific cooperation in Antarctica as according 'with the interests of science and the progress of all mankind'.

These themes are embedded in the first nine Articles of the Treaty. Article 1 emphasizes the demilitarized nature of Antarctica, while Article V prohibits nuclear explosions and disposal of nuclear waste in the territory. Article VI confirms that the area to which the Treaty applies is to be south of 60° South Latitude, including all ice shelves and islands. Articles II and III promote freedom of scientific investigation and cooperation. The non-sovereign status of Antarctica is underlined by Article IV, which freezes claims to the continent, and is reinforced in Article VIII which restates national signatory jurisdiction over their inspectors and scientific personnel in Antarctica. The right of inspections is outlined in Article VII, while Article IX describes the Antarctic Treaty Consultative Parties, and establishes regular Antarctic Treaty Consultative Meetings for the signatory states.

The Treaty is now both the founding document and the lynchpin of a series of legal documents which together comprise the Antarctic Treaty System (ATS). These include the *Convention for the Conservation of Antarctic Seals 1972*,[2] the *Convention on the Conservation of Antarctic Marine Living Resources 1980*[3] (CCAMLR), and the *Protocol on Environmental Protection to the Antarctic Treaty 1991*[4] (PEPAT).

Effectively, there are three groups of signatory parties to the Antarctic Treaty. The first two groups are the Antarctic Treaty Consultative Parties (ATCP) composed of the twelve original signatory states (SS1), and the sixteen other states that signed the Treaty in subsequent years (SS2). The third group is made up of the Non-Consultative Parties. It is the ATCP states that have taken the initiative in formulating policy for Antarctica through their regular meetings. While the non-sovereign status of Antarctica means that the ATCP states can only create policy for their own nationals, the consensual nature of decision-making and cumulative impact of these policy decisions essentially means that these states provide de facto governance for the continent. By contrast, the latter group of twenty Non-Consultative Parties, while adhering to the ATS and the policy decisions generated by the ATCP, have purely observer status at the ATCP meetings and are not eligible to participate in decision-making.

Until very recently, the ATS has lacked permanent bureaucratic infrastructure. Although the idea had been mooted for some years, it was only in 2003 that a Secretariat for the Antarctic Treaty was established under the authority of the ATCP. The Secretariat is charged with facilitating the annual meetings of the ATCPs and the Committee for Environmental Protection (CEP), supporting both the Antarctic Treaty Consultative Meeting (ATCM) and the CEP, and providing a permanent administrative, record-keeping and information link between the parties in the periods between the meetings.[5] The CEP gives advice and makes recommendations to the PEPAT parties. Another key body in the ATS regime is the Scientific Committee on Antarctic Research (SCAR). It has observer status at ATCM and CEP meetings and 'provides independent scientific advice as requested in a variety of fields, particularly on environmental and conservation matters.'[6]

3.   Antarctic Tourism

Globalisation's impact has been felt everywhere on Earth and in Antarctica one of its key manifestations is in tourism. The growing numbers of visitors and tourist vessels provide ample evidence of the attraction of the frozen continent to travellers from all over the world. Their numbers have increased exponentially from the early 1980s thanks to increased accessibility of Antarctica, particularly during the November-March tourist season. Not only have there been steep annual increases in the total number of tourists, but there has also been geographic expansion of the sites they explore, and growth in both the number and size of sea-borne vessels that carry tourists to Antarctica. Along with these increases in tourism, diversification is also occurring with more visitors engaging in a range of activities, including kayaking, diving, skiing and mountain-climbing. The tourist invasion shows no signs of abating, and the economic importance of tourism is apparent from Herr's assertion that 'in dollar terms, the value of the tourism industry makes it second only to fisheries as the most lucrative commercial use of Antarctic resources.'[7] Indeed, Haase states that Antarctica has now entered 'an era which will be dominated by tourism as the main human activity and resource user in Antarctica.'[8]

Antarctic tourism presents a real dilemma for the ATS because it involves so many difficult, inter-connected issues. These include: the problem of non-parties and lack of compliance with ATS tourism regulations; vessel-borne pollution; degradation of Antarctic sites caused by cumulative tourist visitations; contamination by tourists of sites not yet investigated by scientists; disruption of scientific programmes; the introduction of non-indigenous animals, plants or micro-organisms; increased likelihood of aviation and maritime emergencies in the airspace and waters surrounding Antarctica; environmental hazards arising from land, air and sea-based accidents; and pressures to establish land-based tourism infrastructure.[9]

Tourism, then, represents a plethora of challenges for the ATS. Tourism is not specifically mentioned in the Treaty, and it was only in subsequent years that the signatory states identified the need to address the issue. Consequently, ATCMs have since 1966 issued tourism-specific regulations and recommendations.[10] However, the unique nature of Antarctic governance has created a disjunctive situation when applied to tourism. Nationals from signatory states who visit Antarctica are subject to the ATS regime promulgated by their states. Non-signatory state tourists, however, are not. Similarly, there is a disparity in compliance requirements in relation to the tourist companies that operate Antarctica travels, and the vessels that transport air-borne or sea-borne visitors to the continent. As private commercial entities, not only are the tourist companies and vessels not themselves parties to the *Antarctic Treaty*, but there is no requirement that they be registered in a state that is a party to the Treaty. Tourist companies registered in a signatory state and vessels flagged to those states would be required to comply with the state's domestic legislation and regulations relating to Antarctica; third party companies and vessels are not bound in any such way.

Nor is there significant industry self-regulation of Antarctic activities. Although the International Association of Antarctic Tour Operators (IAATO), was established in 1991 and now comprises more than 100 members, membership of the association is not mandatory for Antarctic tour operators. IAATO lists its objectives as operating 'within the parameters of the Antarctic Treaty System', and adhering to the Guidance for Visitors to the Antarctic and 'Guidance for Those Organizing and Conducting Tourism and Non-governmental Activities in the Antarctic, as adopted by the Antarctic Treaty System'.[11] While it is laudable that IAATO attempts to guide its members' actions in this way, it should be noted that there are no enforcement mechanisms, and the only apparent sanction for members who breach these objectives is to reduce their membership status to 'probationary'.[12] There is an uneasy tension, then, between the commercial goals of the tour operators who rely upon exploitation of Antarctica as a wilderness resource, and the environmental values of conservation and protection of Antarctica as a wilderness territory. Nevertheless, Murray and Jabour note that IAATO has established itself as a 'responsible actor', indicated by the 'regular endorsements' it receives from national programmes and by 'the fact that 'several [Treaty] Parties...have initiated the practice of denying visits [to their bases] by non-IAATO members''.[13]

Enforcement, though, remains difficult. Beck notes the gap between the issuing of regulations by ATCPs and their enforcement, arguing that ATPs 'though appreciating the hortatory ('should') and mandatory ('must') nature of various recommendations, have relied upon persuasion and exhortation rather than compulsion.'[14] Adding to the difficulties, supervision of tourists in the Antarctic region is essentially dependent on tour operators themselves. And industry self-regulation is beset with the same problem that bedevils regime compliance - free-riders who exist outside the regime and are not subject to any penalties for non-compliance, but who benefit from the presence of such a regime and compliant parties because that regime contributes to the sustainability of the resource (Antarctica) from which their commercial activities are generated and economic profits derived.

Pollution arising from tourist vessels, and degradation of sites through cumulative tourists visits comprise another set of problems. Zovko notes that, given the swell of tourist vessels in the Southern Ocean, 'the possibility of a grave vessel-sourced pollution incident is not only likely, but inevitable.'[15] The *Exxon Valdez* spill in March 1989 and the sinking in the same year of the Argentinean supply ship, the *Bahia Paraiso*, did nothing to quell fears about a similar disaster waiting to happen in the Antarctic area.

Maritime and aviation emergencies and accidents causing environmental hazards are, thus, two critical sources of pollution. The expansion of Antarctic tourism significantly increases the likelihood of accidents and emergencies. This was demonstrated in the sinking of the *M/S Explorer* in November 2007.[16] Although there were no fatalities, an unknown amount of fuel was spilled in the Southern Ocean, making this one of the most serious shipping accidents in the region and causing as yet unquantified damage to the environment. Until the adoption in 2005 of Annex VI (Liability Arising From Environmental Emergencies) to PEPAT there was no clear policy about such incidents, and although the Annex is 'somewhat problematic'[17] it does represent progress in providing a regimen for Antarctica. It also underlines a continuing problem in tourist emergency rescue and humanitarian relief efforts. Although five states share responsibility as Rescue Coordination Centres for Search and Rescue programmes in Antarctica, some of the burden has had to be borne by national scientific programmes which had 'to divert scarce resources for emergency assistance or search and rescue facilities.'[18]

Pollution also arises from human contact with an environment, particularly repeated contact in a specific site. Industry statistics 'show that about 85 percent of tourists visit Antarctica's top 20 landing sites, all of them on the 800-mile-long Antarctic Peninsula, which has the continent's mildest climate and most diverse wildlife.'[19] Such repeated human contact within a small area must inevitably raise questions about how much contact the area can sustain before it is irredeemably degraded. In the tourist industry this point of no return is known as the carrying capacity - 'a point beyond which further levels of visitation or development would lead to an unacceptable deterioration of the physical environment and of the visitor's experience'. The authors note that carrying capacity plays a pivotal role in considerations of the impact of tourism because it intervenes 'in the relationship between visitor and resource.'[20]

Carrying capacity is also obviously of concern in a scientific context. While any use of a site will result in human impacts, the need for careful management is imperative when sites are both limited in scale and intensively used by tourists, as in the Antarctic Peninsula. Yet such activities are not adequately captured, evaluated, monitored or managed by the existing ATS regulatory frameworks. Annex I of PEPAT does provide protocols to address human impacts on the environment through its Environmental Impact process. This process applies to all activities that have more than a 'minor or transitory impact' in the Antarctic Treaty area.[21] For those activities meeting that criterion, an Initial Environmental Evaluation (IEE) must be prepared. If the IEE indicates that the proposed activity will have more than a minor or transitory impact, then a Comprehensive Environmental Evaluation (CEE) is required to be prepared. The CEE must be circulated to all PEPAT parties with a 90-day period being allowed for comments, and then forwarded to the CEP and the next ATCM.[22] If a CEE is approved, then procedures 'shall be put in place, including appropriate monitoring of key environmental indicators, to assess and verify the impact of any activity that proceeds following the completion of a Comprehensive Environmental Evaluation.'[23]

However, there are three key problems with this process. Firstly, cumulative impacts have been neither properly researched, nor subject to rigorous regulation, particularly at sites that are intensively used.[24] Secondly, neither CEP nor the ATCM have decision-making authority in relation to the CEE; their role in this process is simply to give advice to the government that has prepared the CEE. As Joyner puts it, 'the ultimate arbiter of what will be done on the continent belongs to individual national governments…this procedure contradicts what should be a comprehensive approach.'[25] And, thirdly, not only is the Environmental Impact Assessment (EIA) process compromised by lack of appropriate scientific rigour in decision-making and deference to national governments, but State Parties adherence to monitoring and reporting requirements after a CEE has been approved leave much to be desired.[26]

These problems are compounded by the need to achieve consensus among parties in the ATS in order to maintain the regime. The 'softly, softly' approach that has dominated diplomatic activity in the regime has proved its worth in the longevity, stability, and enhanced functioning of the ATS, but it comes at a price. Technological advances and the pressures wrought by globalisation often outstrip the capacity of the slow and careful decision-making processes to keep pace with them, and the need to maintain consensus and keep a cooperative balance between the parties can inhibit much-needed change.

Additionally, there are problems within the ATS regime itself in relation to tourism. Enzenbacher lists these as:

> the lack of tourism management expertise on Treaty delegations, the low priority tourism has been given historically as a policy issue, the lack of agreement on how tourism should be addressed, varying levels of direct involvement and financial gain among Member States and the evermore demanding remit facing Antarctic policy-makers.[27]

Something of that division can be seen in the debate over permanent land-based facilities for tourism, a development that would obviously exacerbate the problems associated with the increasing number of travellers in Antarctica. There are currently very limited facilities available, but Bastmeijer, Lamers and Harcha note that there is interest in the issue 'in view of the fast developments in the Antarctic tourism industry.'[28] Since 2004 the issue has been very much on the international agenda, but there is no clear mandate for the ATCMs to issue regulations about such facilities. Far from it. Differences in opinion on the issue are evident from the stances taken by, for instance, the New Zealand, Norwegian, Argentinean, and Chilean governments. But it is not simply that signatory states have different opinions about permanent land-based facilities that prevent explicit, legally binding decisions being made about the issue. Worryingly, Bastmeijer, Lamers and Harcha comment that

> the discussions are not based on clear definitions, inventories of existing facilities, potential future developments and arguments for and against these developments. A clear overview and comparative analysis of the various management options is also missing.[29]

The ad hoc nature of decision-making about tourism at ATCMs and the impression that the ATCM 'is not able to address the various more strategic questions'[30] suggest strongly that this is an area where a clash between differing national and international interests and different philosophical approaches to the status of Antarctica are leading to a stasis in decision-making and leaving a dangerous vacuum in policy and governance of the continent.

All fragile environments are impacted by tourism and in that sense Antarctica is no different from other wilderness destinations which have similarly experienced tourism development.[31] Where Antarctica is different, though, is in its particular place in the global ecosystem. Thanks to its inhospitable nature as the coldest, driest and windiest place on earth,[32] the continent has no indigenous human population, and for centuries was free from human habitation. Although that latter situation changed in the twentieth century, Antarctica today is in a unique position as a bellwether environment. Additionally, Antarctica has been described both as a 'scientific laboratory'[33] and as a 'frozen time capsule' because of its 'role as an historical archive of climatic and pollution conditions in other parts of the world'[34], making it possible to retrieve from ice core samples information about global environments prior to pre-industrial times. Antarctica's place in the current and future global ecosystems is also paramount because 'of the region's integral role in global environmental systems and its influence upon world climates, oceans, and sea levels.'[35] As the repository of approximately 70 percent of the world's freshwater resources (in the form of icebergs and ice-sheets), Antarctica's future is vital to the fate of humankind.

That there are few wilderness areas on Earth, though, adds to the attractiveness of the remaining few for tourists seeking a destination and an experience out of the ordinary. The irony and the tragedy of this is that, as Smith notes, such areas are 'under attack in the guise of *ecotourism*', sometimes referred to as *eco*nomic tourism 'because it often merely means that tourism is being pushed, for entrepreneurial gain, ever deeper into isolated and heretofore little-visited terrain' - a phenomenon that further jeopardises the already fragile environments.[36]

Not all impacts of tourism are negative or harmful, though. Certainly, in the Antarctic a substantial part of the concern that has been expressed in recent decades about the growth in tourism can be linked to the lack of a comprehensive tourism policy under the ATS, and reactive rather than proactive stances as outcomes of ATCMs. However, that is a failure of the governance system for the Antarctic - itself a function of the non-sovereign status of Antarctica and condominium approach of the Treaty - and not solely attributable to the activities of tourists themselves.

There can be positive impacts of tourism in Antarctica. For instance, there are benefits in exposing to Antarctica people who are not part of national scientific expeditions. The increasing numbers of tourists who visit Antarctica get a first-hand experience of the extraordinary nature of the continent and can see for themselves the importance of preserving the environment. In this context, those tourists are potentially a real and very potent asset as they can act as change agents in civil society by educating others about the territory, promoting the benefits of protecting Antarctica as a common good, and helping lobby governments to respect both the continent's non-sovereign status and its importance in the global environmental system. The politicisation effect of such an experience should not be under-estimated. As has been demonstrated in the successful campaigns to ban land mines and cluster bombs, civil society has an increasingly powerful presence and impact in the trans-national politics of the twenty-first century. The experiential nature of tourism in the Antarctic, therefore, must not be undermined by greater regulation. On the contrary, it is possible to conceive of a complementary and mutually reinforcing relationship between the experiential interaction and the endogenous effects of regulation which could engender positive and lasting impacts on tourists' beliefs about and behaviours concerning the Antarctic environment.

Another benefit of Antarctic tourism may lie in the generation of an additional revenue stream for scientific research. As well as becoming 'ambassadors' for a wilderness area such as Antarctica, tourists may also become sources of conservation revenue. Maher, Steel and McIntosh comment that 'tourists become emotionally attached to an area and will thus contribute funds to protect it or improve its conservation status.'[37] Cessford notes that tourists are particularly interested in visits to scientific stations, something which allows the scientists 'more direct advocacy of the research being done to an interested audience' and 'provides opportunities for generating revenue from postal and souvenir services'.[38] Additionally, 'tour vessels have provided transportation of staff and materials for management and research purposes.'[39]

Tourism can also play an important role in providing other types of benefits to scientists and scientific research programmes in Antarctica. According to Murray and Jabour, independent expeditions have proved their utility in two regards, assisting

> the Australian program with scientific work and by demonstrating the capabilities of fixed-wing aircraft for Antarctic use. Similarly, as a nascent commercial operation, ANI proved the possibilities of blue-ice runways.[40]

It also needs to be acknowledged that it is not just tourists and tourist vessels that can have a negative impact on the environment. Scientists, simply by their presence, also leave their mark on the environment, and the expanding number of scientists and permanent bases in Antarctica has a proportionally greater impact on the territory. Ironically, it was the advent of large-scale tourism that led to the clean-up of notoriously polluted scientific bases.[41]

Given the significant and increasing number of visitors coming to Antarctica, and the pressing number of inter-related issues arising from their presence, tourism is undoubtedly one of the greatest challenges that the ATCPs face and one that must be addressed as urgently as possible.

4.   The Future of Antarctica

No less problematic than tourism is the question of the future of Antarctica. That issue flared dramatically in 1982 when the then-Prime Minister of Malaysia criticised the extant membership of the ATCP for its exclusive, secretive and unaccountable nature, and urged the United Nations to consider the 'common heritage of all the nations of this planet....the largest of which is the continent of Antarctica'.[42] That the ATCP were sensitive to the charges of being an aristocratic club is evident from the expanded and internationalized membership from 1983 onwards. Baslar comments that the 'big brothers of the Third World were accepted in order to dissipate the club's notorious image', and that with 'the acceptance of the most populated prestigious members of the Third Division, the ATS turned out to be an oligarchic league composed of three-quarters of the world's population.'[43]

However, while the membership of the Treaty may have expanded, the question of the future of Antarctica remained in limbo. The United Nations General Assembly considered the question during the 1980s. Joyner notes that 'many governments not party to the Antarctic Treaty tended to view Antarctica politically and legally through the lens of developing countries, particularly on issues that affected their own socio-economic concerns.'[44] These concerns included a focus on the massive, untapped natural resources of Antarctica and the importance of the continent in the global ecosystem. They also extended into the legal and political realms with the vexed question of Antarctica's legal status, the privileged decision-making role of the SS1 states (akin to the position of the five permanent members of the United Nations Security Council) in the ATS, and the inequitable and unrepresentative nature of the decision-making.

Antarctica's future remained on the United Nations table for another decade but, after expansion of the ATS membership in the 1980s, was revisited less frequently and less heatedly. However, while the membership issue has not raised headlines for some time, the question of who controls the Antarctic agenda has not been laid to rest, and is of particular salience for the

21st century because it is integrally linked to the future of Antarctica and how that will be determined.

The common heritage of mankind conceptualisation of Antarctica is not the only one that has been suggested. United Nations involvement in Antarctica was advocated strongly in the first two decades after that institution's establishment, the most frequent proposal being use of the Trusteeship Council to administer Antarctica. In 1972 the Second World Congress on National Parks argued that the continent and surrounding ocean should become the first world park, overseen by the United Nations.[45] A key element of that proposal - the notion of special protections for particular areas in Antarctica - was incorporated into PEPAT through Annex V. New Zealand, one of the founding ATCPs, took up the issue of a world park and in 1975 formally proposed that Antarctica be designated as the first World Park.[46] Another conceptualisation for Antarctica is as a natural reserve of intrinsic value to be managed by the ATCPs within the construct of the ATS.

Essentially, then, there are three different concepts - common heritage, world park, natural reserve - that have been suggested as appropriate for adoption in Antarctica. What has been lacking, though, is a sustained, rigorous, open, and accessible debate between the proponents of each about the merits of the different proposals and what they would involve in terms of management of Antarctica and its resources.

A. Common Heritage

The common heritage of mankind concept is derived from a speech made by the Maltese Ambassador, Arvid Pardo, at the UN General Assembly in 1967. Pardo's speech was focused on the legal status of the seabed and, in that context, he introduced the idea of an area beyond the national jurisdiction of any state that was common to, or the heritage of, all humankind.[47] This skeleton of an idea was fleshed out in the General Assembly's subsequent 1970 *Declaration of Principles Governing the Seabed and the Ocean Floor and the Subsoil Thereof, Beyond the Limits of National Jurisdiction*. The Declaration enunciated the four key principles and precepts of the common heritage concept: an area or territory sited beyond the limits of any state's jurisdiction, not subject to appropriation by a state, over which no state could claim or exercise sovereignty rights, and in which area an international regime could be established that would govern any activities relating to exploration or exploitation of the resources of the area.

The concept soon gained traction. The phrase 'common interests of all mankind' was incorporated into the 1967 *Treaty on Principles Governing the Activities of States in the Exploration and Use of Outer Space, Including the Moon and other Celestial Bodies*, and 'the common heritage of mankind' became the guiding principle of regulation of 'the Area' in the 1982 *United Nations Convention on the Law of the Sea*.

The common heritage concept is based on a number of rationales which relate to five specific premises: the idea of a common interest; non-renewable resources; scientific value and research; financial value; and limited availability. Holmila notes that the 'first and foremost characteristic of the common heritage of mankind is that its purpose is to advance public or common interest', notably in respect of being 'regimes that have a particular importance to economic development and to the world of science.'[48] The second rationale is the non-renewability of resources that comprise the common heritage which requires 'balancing the powers and interests of states'[49] so that the resources are not exploited to the point of exhaustion and will be retained for future generations. The value of scientific research conducted in the common heritage areas is the third rationale. The common heritage areas are unlike any others on Earth or in space and, therefore, the information that can be garnered from scientific research at these sites is something in which everyone can be said to have a stake - it is scientific research that is extraordinarily valuable for all of humankind. The fourth rationale is the incredible financial value of the resources of the common heritage area, although no exact figure can be placed on these because the extent of those resources is not yet known. The fifth and final rationale relates to the limited availability of the resources, not just in the sense of their non-renewability, but also due to the fact that their 'exploitation requires vast amounts of capital, both monetary and technological, that only a very few and selected states have', hence they should 'not be subject to free competition'.[50]

The central question about justice in relation to the common heritage issue is where does justice lie? Should the common heritage concept be used to exploit Antarctic resources with preference given to developing states, thus facilitating development of the Global South and enhancing the prospects of equality between Global South and Global North? Or should the common heritage concept be used to effect sustainable development of Antarctic resources, balancing both intra- and inter-generational justice? Or does justice consist of allowing states equally the freedom to exploit Antarctic resources to gain maximum profits for themselves, their corporations, and their citizens? There are different aspects of justice at play in these questions, different perceptions of entitlement, and very different outcomes for Antarctica that would be generated. As Shackelford has said, with considerable understatement, developing 'and developed nations disagree over the extent of international regulation required to equitably manage commons resources.'[51]

In the first conceptualisation, Antarctica presents as a territory of infinite resources - a site of abundance and potential solution to the world's scarcity of resources. Benefit-sharing in this conceptualisation is about equitable sharing of the extracted resources of Antarctica to help maintain humankind. The enormous gap between Global North and Global South could, in this scheme, be reduced, potentially saving the lives of the hundreds of thousands of people in developing countries who die each year of easily preventable diseases, and giving new hope and real opportunities for a better life to the millions who live in abject poverty. This conceptualisation of the common heritage is about making concrete the basic necessities of Maslow's hierarchy of needs, and achieving the promises of dignity and equality enshrined in human rights instruments such as the 1948 *Universal Declaration of Human Rights*. It is also a conceptualisation that would necessarily endorse a regime permitting considerable commercial exploitation of Antarctic resources in order to gain the significant capital injections that would be needed to address Global South inequalities.

In the second conceptualisation, the common heritage notion is a vehicle for sustainable development, and justice within and between generations. Although Bosselmann notes that the 'meaning and significance of sustainable development are highly contested', nevertheless 'most definitions of SD reflect the dual goal of intra- and intergenerational justice and the means of integrating environmental, social and economic policies.'[52] This common heritage scheme would have some overlap with the first, insofar as engaging with inequalities would be required to achieve the goal of intra-generational justice. However, the inequalities highlighted would not necessarily be those of the Global South as a bloc. They might as easily be the inequalities that exist in Global North states where both absolute as well as relative poverty is present. This conceptualisation of the common heritage would allow some commercial exploitation of the continent, but would indubitably place rigorous limitations and constraints upon Antarctic resources in order to preserve the commons for future generations.

As Shaw notes, 'a common heritage regime...would strictly regulate exploration and exploitation, would establish management mechanisms and would employ the criterion of equity in distributing the benefits of such activity.'[53] However, equity is, like sustainable development, a contestable concept and compatible with widely varying interpretations. Thus, it is possible to conceive of equity within a common heritage framework being viewed as a mechanism that is applied within the framework of different state ideologies and with the aim of consistency with those ideologies and their national priorities. Thus, the third conceptualisation of the common heritage gives rein to the idea that there cannot be justice without liberty. In this scheme Antarctica is a site of resources that should be readily available to all states without favour or preference. The underlying premise is that states have differing political and economic ideologies and should, even within the parameters of an international regime, have the freedom to pursue their own ideas of justice in relation to exploitation of the continent's resources. The international regime overseeing exploitation of Antarctica's resources would be required to be sufficiently flexible and free from undue regulation to allow states to express their ideologically-oriented justice preferences in an equitable sharing of benefits derived from the resources. The question of who benefits from the equity criterion would, then, be viewed and determined by each state through their individual ideological prism, and applied domestically or internationally, solely, or in bilateral or multilateral distribution regimes as they saw fit.

B. World Park

A second proposal that has been made about Antarctica's future status is for the continent to become a world park. In this scheme Antarctica would become a protected area, managed under similar regimes to other protected areas (like national parks) in different parts of the world. The idea was very much a product of its times. In 1972 *The Convention Concerning the Protection of the World Cultural and Natural Heritage* was adopted by the UN Economic and Social Council and came into force in 1975. By 2009 it had been ratified by 186 states.[54] Like the common heritage concept, the idea of world heritage includes recognition of universal value or importance for all of humankind and suggests that the territory in question transcends national boundaries, and should be managed in accordance with a particular regime. Unlike the common heritage concept, though, the world heritage concept is strongly committed to permanent protection of a site, and would not countenance commercial exploitation of its resources. Maintaining the integrity of a site in this scheme is paramount to ensure that it is guarded and protected for the future.

The world park proposal was based on similar ideas about protection of Antarctica, and on prioritising environmental values. As Hammer puts it, '[t]he paramount objective of a protected area is, according to the internationally accepted definition, conservation.'[55] Accordingly, a World Conservation Strategy 'which identified Antarctica and the Southern Ocean as a priority for international action'[56] was developed by a number of non-governmental organizations, the World Wildlife Fund, and the United Nations Environmental Programme.

However, the world park proposal was defeated by the consulting parties, some on the grounds of a world park concept being 'inconsistent with their position on sovereignty', while others 'flatly refused to foreclose forever the possibility that Antarctica's mineral resources might one day be utilised.'[57]

Baslar suggests that there is considerable tension between a world park idea and the common heritage of humankind idea. A world park proposal would, he says, be 'inherently hostile to any exploitation activities apart from the exploitation for scientific research', while the common heritage idea 'regards the continent as a territory of instrumental value'.[58]

Both proposals share an acceptance of Antarctica's prime importance for the future, and view Antarctica as conferring benefits for the human race. However, the benefits they perceive are derived from very different visions of Antarctica; Antarctica as a territory necessarily in stasis versus Antarctica as a producer of needed resources.

The world park concept is one that has been heard less often in the last decade, but the idea of guardianship inherent in it has become more important in Antarctica. Berkman suggests that 'nations have begun transcending the next level into 'global stewardship', where they work together under a realm of common authority without 'asserting, supporting or denying' their sovereign claims.'[59]

C. Natural Reserve

The third proposal for Antarctica's future is as a natural reserve. This proposal is derived from the wording of Article 2 of PEPAT in which the parties 'designate Antarctica as a natural reserve, devoted to peace and science'. This concept of a natural reserve shares some characteristics with both the common heritage and world park proposals in that it acknowledges Antarctica's unique status in the global ecosystem. It also overlaps with the world park proposal in that it prioritizes environmental values. For instance, Article 2 of PEPAT uses the phrasing 'comprehensive protection of the Antarctic environment' to denote the over-arching nature of protection under this agreement. Similarly, Article 3(1) refers to 'the intrinsic value of Antarctica, including its wilderness and aesthetic values', as well as to the importance of the scientific research conducted in Antarctica to 'understanding the global environment'.

Where the natural reserve proposal is distinctively different from the previous two proposals, though, is in its acknowledgement of an existing regime (the ATS), and its requirement that the natural park proposal fits within the boundaries of that regime. There is no suggestion in PEPAT that any other regime should supplant the ATS, nor that any governance bodies other than those established under the ATS should be involved in this regime. Consequently, the natural park proposal further embeds the ATCPs as the managers of Antarctica and decision-makers about its future. Hence, PEPAT reiterates core ideas of the Treaty about the importance of scientific research and peace in Antarctica, but also incorporates into the Protocol subsequent developments (such as the 'designation of Antarctica as a Special Conservation Area'[60] and the establishment of CCAMLR) of the ATS. It also appropriates some of the language of the common heritage concept and piggybacks that onto the idea of the ATS regime. For instance, in the Preamble to the Protocol the Parties agree that 'the development of a comprehensive regime for the protection of the Antarctic environment and dependent and associated ecosystems is in the interest of mankind as a whole'.

It is possible to see in the natural park proposal a confirmation of Berkman's suggestion that global stewardship is the evolving meta-principle in relation to the continent and the ATS. The Protocol's Preamble affirms that Antarctica has a 'special legal and political status', and that the ATCPs have a 'special responsibility' to 'ensure that all activities in Antarctica are consistent with the purposes and principles of the Antarctic Treaty', a reference to the freezing of sovereign claims to Antarctica established under the Treaty, and the need for the signatory states to act in a manner consonant with the eco-protectionist ATS instruments they have committed themselves to. As that includes PEPAT's own prohibition in Article 7 of any mineral activities other than for scientific research, it presents a formidable challenge to common heritage ideas concerning resource exploitation in the continent.

What the natural park proposal does is to confirm, from the perspective of ATCPs, the appropriateness of the ATS as the regime for Antarctica into the future. It does not propose easing of the membership requirements to make it a more inclusive regime, nor does it invite oversight by or cooperation with an existing global institution (such as the United Nations) in order to give it more legitimacy and credibility in proposing and sustaining a regime for the Antarctic that is 'in the interest of mankind as a whole.' Rather, it assumes that the ATS will continue indefinitely as the arbiter of Antarctica's fate.

There is no clear consensus about the way forward for Antarctica's future. The common heritage proposal is particularly vulnerable to scholarly disagreement about what the fundamentals of the concept are. Holmila has described it as a 'vague concept that is hard to describe in terms of legal rules',[61] Mason calls it 'an idealistic expression of a goal of universal justice',[62] while Suter criticises the common heritage concept for its lack of precision and for reopening controversies over territorial claims, suggesting it should be dropped in favour of a new concept that retains the common heritage focus on protection of the environment, but does not employ the common heritage nomenclature.[63]

Undoubtedly, the territorial claims aspect is a sticking point in the common heritage concept for some ATCPs with claims in Antarctica. Potential loss of claimed territory under a common heritage regime represents sufficient reason not to move forward with that proposal for the future, but to prefer the natural park concept. The privileging of developing states in the first iteration of the common heritage concept may be another reason for other (developed) ATCPs to prefer a different proposal. And perceived encroachment on national sovereignty in both the common heritage and world park proposals may be a further aspect that is distasteful to some states.

5.   Conclusion

Given that there is no universal agreement about the common heritage proposal and uncertain support for the world park proposal, it would seem that in the absence of an alternative that can gain strong support from states, particularly the ATCPs, the natural reserve proposal will by default become the blueprint for Antarctica's future. In that context, Francioni has posed the important question of whether the natural reserve concept 'is likely to be universally accepted by the international community as a whole or will rather remain limited to the Antarctic Treaty Parties.'[64]

The three proposals examined here for Antarctica's future are not the only ones suggested for Antarctica's future. These proposals must compete with the commercial visions of entrepreneurs and developers, particularly in the tourism industry, for whom Antarctica represents the Klondike of the twenty-first century. Unless and until the ATCPs can reach agreement amongst themselves about Antarctica's future and apply that vision through more robust governance mechanisms, the combined pressures of commercialisation, privatisation, and globalisation will likely be harder and harder to resist. The ultimate test for the ATS will be to resolve these challenges before they move beyond the capability of the Antarctic governance bodies to control them.

Notes

[1] The Antarctic Treaty, Washington, 1959, 402 UNTS 1961 72. Henceforth, the Treaty.

[2] Convention for the Conservation of Antarctic Seals, 29 UST 44 1, TIAS no.8826.

[3] Convention on the Conservation of Antarctic Marine Living Resources, 1980 19 ILM 841.

[4] Protocol on Environmental Protection to the Antarctic Treaty, 1991 30 ILM 1461. Hereafter, PEPAT.

[5] P Vigni, 'The Secretariat of the Antarctic Treaty: Achievements and Weaknesses Three Years After its Establishment', *Antarctica: Legal and Environmental Challenges for the Future*, British Institute of International & Comparative Law, London, 2007, pp.17-19.

[6] Scientific Committee on Antarctic Research, *The Antarctic Treaty System: An Introduction*, Viewed 4 May, 2009, <http://www.scar.org/treaty/>.

[7] R Herr, 'The Regulation of Antarctic Tourism: A Study in Regime Effectiveness', *Governing the Antarctic: The Effectiveness and Legitimacy of the Antarctic Treaty System*, Cambridge University Press, Cambridge, 1996, p.205.

[8] D Haase, 'Too Much Pressure on Thin Ice?' Antarctic Tourism and Regulatory Considerations', *Polarforschung*, Vol. 75, No.1, 2005, p.22.

[9] C Joyner, *Governing the Frozen Commons: The Antarctic Regime and Environmental Protection,* University of South Carolina, Columbia, 1998, pp.208-212.

[10] P Beck, 'Regulating One of the Last Tourism Frontiers: Antarctica', *Applied Geography*, Vol. 10, 1990, p.345.

[11] See IAATO, *About IIATO: Objectives*, Viewed May 24, 2009, <http://www.iaato.org/objectives.html>.

[12] C Murray & J Jabour, 'Independent Expeditions and Antarctic Tourism Policy', *Polar Record*, Vol. 40, No. 215, 2004, p.310.

[13] ibid, p.309.

[14] P Beck, 'Managing Antarctic Tourism: A Front-Burner Issue', *Annals of Tourism Research*, Vol. 21, No. 2, p.379.

[15] I Zovko, 'Vessel-Sourced Pollution in the Southern Ocean', *Antarctica: Legal and Environmental Challenges for the Future*, British Institute of International & Comparative Law, London, 2007, p.193.

[16] N Muller, 'Alarm Bells Sound for Antarctic Tourist Vessels', *The Valparaiso Times*, 6 May 2009, Viewed 28 May, 2009, <http://www.valparaisotimes.cl/content/view/524/388/>.

[17] L de La Fayette, 'Responding to Environmental Damage in Antarctica', *Antarctica: Legal and Environmental Challenges for the Future*, British Institute of International & Comparative Law, London, 2007, p.110.

[18] P Beck, 'Regulating One of the Last Tourism Frontiers: Antarctica', *Applied Geography*, Vol. 10, 1990, p.350.

[19] B Deutsch, 'Sinking Raises Questions About Antarctic Tourism', *Dallas Morning News*, December 31, 2007, p.3, Viewed October 5, 2009. <http://www.dallasnews.com/sharedcontent/dws/fea/travel/thisweek/stories/DN-antarc_1230tra.State.Edition1.d925de.html >.

[20] B Archer & C Cooper, 'The Positive and Negative Impacts of Tourism', *Global Tourism*, 2nd ed., Butterworth Heinemann, Oxford, 1998, pp. 63-64.

[21] PEPAT, Art 2(1).

[22] PEPAT, Art 3(3) & (4).

[23] PEPAT, Art 5(1).

[24] M Lamers, D Haase & B Amelung, 'Facing The Elements: Analysing Trends in Antarctic Tourism', *Tourism Review*, Vol. 63, No. 1, 2008, p.21.

[25] Joyner, *Governing the Frozen Commons: The Antarctic Regime and Environmental Protection*, p.156.

[26] M Jacobsson, 'The Antarctic Treaty System: Future Challenges', *Antarctica: Legal and Environmental Challenges for the Future*, British Institute of International and Comparative Law, London, 2007, p.11.

[27] D Enzenbacher, 'Antarctic Tourism Policy-Making: Current Challenges and Future Prospects', *Antarctica: Legal and Environmental Challenges for the Future*, British Institute of International & Comparative Law, London, 2007, p.155.

[28] K Bastmeijer, M Lamers & J Harcha, 'Permanent Land-Based Facilities for Tourism In Antarctica: The Need for Regulation', *Receil,* Vol. 17, No. 1, 2008, p.85.

[29] ibid.

[30] K Bastmeijer, 'A Long Term Strategy for Antarctic Tourism: The Key to Decision Making Within the Antarctic Treaty System?', Social Science Research Network, Viewed October 5, 2009, <http://ssrn.com/abstract= 1335091>.

[31] See D Harrison & MF Price, 'Fragile Environments, Fragile Communities? An Introduction', *People and Tourism in Fragile Environments*, John Wiley & Sons, Chichester, 1996, pp.1-18.

[32] V Smith, 'A Sustainable Antarctic: Science and Tourism', *Annals of Tourist Research*, Vol. 21, No. 2, 1994, p.221.

[33] RT Scully & L Kimball, 'Antarctica: Is There Life After Minerals?', *Marine Policy*, April 1989, p.88.

[34] P Beck, 'Antarctica Enters the 1990s: An Overview', *Applied Geography*, Vol. 10, p.248.

[35] ibid.

[36] V Smith, 'Foreword', *People and Tourism in Fragile Environments*, John Wiley & Sons, Chichester, 1996, p.xiv.

[37] P Maher, G. Steel & A McIntosh, 'Antarctica: Tourism, Wilderness, and 'Ambassadorship'', USDA Forest Service Proceedings RMRS-P-27, *Seventh World Wilderness Congress Symposium*, 2003, p.208.

[38] G Cessford, 'Antarctic Tourism – A Frontier for Wilderness Management', *Antarctica in the Environmental Age*, Department of Conservation, Wellington, 1998, pp.27-28.

[39] ibid.

[40] Murray & Jabour, op.cit., 'pp.315-316.

[41] B Deutsch, 'Sinking Raises Questions About Antarctic Tourism', *Dallas Morning News*, December 31, 2007, p.2, Viewed October 5, 2009. <http://www.dallasnews.com/sharedcontent/dws/fea/travel/thisweek/stories/ DN-antarc_1230tra.State.Edition1.d925de.html >.

[42] Dr. M Mohamed, quoted in K Baslar, *The Concept of the Common Heritage of Mankind in International Law,* Marinus Nijhoff Publishers, The Hague, 1998, p.244.

[43] Baslar, op.cit., p.248.

[44] Joyner, *Governing the Frozen Commons: The Antarctic Regime and Environmental Protection*, p.239.

[45] A Gillespie, *Protected Areas and International Environmental Law*, Martinus Nijhoff Publishers, Leiden, 2007, p.15.

[46] G Palmer, *Environmental Politics: A Greenprint for New Zealand*, John McIndoe, Dunedin, 1990, p.77.

[47] See P Payoyo, 'The Common Heritage of Mankind and Global Environmental Governance', Fourth Annual Common Property Conference, IASCP, Philippines, 1993, pp.4-5.

[48] E Holmila, 'Common Heritage of Mankind in the Law of the Sea', *Acta Societatis Martensis*, Vol. 1, 2005, p.193.

[49] ibid.

[50] ibid, p.194.

[51] S Shackelford, 'The Tragedy of the Common Heritage of Mankind', *Stanford Environmental Law Journal*, Vol. 27, No. 27, 2008, p.102.

[52] K Bosselmann, 'The Concept of Sustainable Development', *Environmental Law for a Sustainable Society*, New Zealand Centre for Environmental Law Monograph Series: Vol. 1, New Zealand Centre for Environmental Law, Auckland, 2002, pp.87-88.

[53] M Shaw, *International Law*, 4th ed., Cambridge University Press, Cambridge, 1997, p.362.

[54] UNESCO, World Heritage Convention: Statistics on States Parties, Viewed October 24, 2009, <http://whc.unesco.org/en/statesparties/stat/#sp3>.

[55] T Hammer, 'Protected Areas and Regional Development: Conflict and Opportunities', *Protected Areas and Regional Development in Europe: Towards a New Model for the 21st Century*, Ashgate, Aldershot, 2007, p.21.

[56] P Berkman, *Science Into Policy: Global Lessons From Antarctica*, Academic Press, San Diego, 2002, p.73.

[57] Palmer, op.cit., p.77.

[58] Baslar, op.cit., pp.259, 261.

[59] P Berkman, op.cit., pp.74-75.

[60] Preamble, PEPAT.

[61] Holmila, op.cit., p.190.

[62] The Hon. Sir A Mason, 'The International Concept of Equality of Interest in the Sea as it Affects the Conservation of the Environment and Indigenous Interests', *Land, Rights, Laws: Issues of Native Title*, Vol. 2, Issues Paper No.16, Land Title Research Unit, Australian Institute of Aboriginal and Torres Strait Islander Studies, June 2002, p.4.

[63] K Suter, *Antarctica: Private Property or Public Heritage?*, Pluto Press, Australia, 1991, p.165.

[64] F Francioni, 'Introduction: A Decade of Development in Antarctic International Law', F Francioni & T Scovazzi, (eds), *International Law for Antarctica*, 2nd ed., Kluwer Law International, The Hague, 1996, p.9.

Bibliography

Archer, B. & Cooper, C., 'The Positive and Negative Impacts of Tourism'. *Global Tourism*. 2nd ed., Butterworth Heineman, Oxford, 1998, pp.63-81.

Baslar, K., *The Concept of the Common Heritage of Mankind in International Law*. Martinus Nijhoff Publishers, The Hague, 1998.

Bastmeijer, K., 'A Long Term Strategy for Antarctic Tourism: The Key to Decision Making Within the Antarctic Treaty System?' Social Science Research Network, Viewed October 5, 2009, <http://ssrn.com/abstract= 1335091>.

Bastmeijer, K., Lamers, M. & Harcha, J., Permanent Land-Based Facilities for Tourism In Antarctica: The Need for Regulation'. *Review of European Community and International Environmental Law*. Vol. 17, No. 1, 2008, pp.84-99.

Beck, P., 'Regulating One of the Last Tourism Frontiers: Antarctica'. *Applied Geography*. Vol. 10, 1990, pp.343-356.

——, 'Managing Antarctic Tourism: A Front-Burner Issue'. *Annals of Tourism Research*. Vol. 21, No. 2, 1994, pp.375-386.

——, 'Antarctica Enters the 1990s: An Overview'. *Applied Geography*. Vol. 10, 1990, pp.247-263.

Berkman, P., *Science Into Policy: Global Lessons From Antarctica*. Academic Press, San Diego, 2002.

Bosselmann, K. & Grinlinton, D., (eds), *Environmental Law for a Sustainable Society*. New Zealand Centre for Environmental Law Monograph Series, Vol. 1, Auckland, 2002.

Cessford, G., 'Antarctic Tourism: A Frontier for Wilderness Management'. *Antarctica in the Environmental Age*. Department of Conservation, Wellington, 1998.

Deutsch, B., 'Sinking Raises Questions About Antarctic Tourism'. *Dallas Morning News*. December 31, 2007, p.3, Viewed October 5, 2009. <http://www.dallasnews.com/sharedcontent/dws/fea/travel/thisweek/stories/DN-antarc_1230tra.State.Edition1.d925de.html >.

Dodds, K., *Geopolitics in Antarctica*. John Wiley & Sons Ltd, Chichester, 1997.

Enzenbacher, D., 'Antarctic Tourism Policy-Making: Current Challenges and Future Prospects'. *Antarctica: Legal and Environmental Challenges for the Future*. British Institute of International & Comparative Law, London, 2007.

Francioni, F., 'Introduction: A Decade of Development in Antarctic International Law'. *International Law for Antarctica*. 2nd ed., Kluwer Law International, The Hague, 1996, pp.1-16.

Gillespie, A., *Protected Areas and International Environmental Law*. Martinus Nijhoff Publishers, Leiden, 2007.

Haase, D., 'Too Much Pressure on Thin Ice?' Antarctic Tourism and Regulatory Considerations'. *Polarforschung*. Vol. 75, No. 1, 2005, pp.21-27.

Hammer, T., 'Protected Areas and Regional Development: Conflict and Opportunities'. *Protected Areas and Regional Development in Europe: Towards a New Model for the 21st Century*. Ashgate, Aldershot, 2007.

Harrison, D. & Price, M.F., 'Fragile Environments, Fragile Communities? An Introduction'. *People and Tourism in Fragile Environments*. John Wiley & Sons, Chichester, 1996.

Herr, R., 'The Regulation of Antarctic Tourism: A Study in Regime Effectiveness'. *Governing the Antarctic: The Effectiveness and Legitimacy of the Antarctic Treaty System*. Cambridge University Press, Cambridge, 1996.

Holmila, E., 'Common Heritage of Mankind in the Law of the Sea'. *Acta Societatis Martensis*. Vol. 1, 2005, pp.187-205.

——, *About IIATO: Objectives*, Viewed 24 May, 2009, <http://www.iaato.org/objectives.html>.

Joyner, C., *Governing the Frozen Commons: The Antarctic Regime and Environmental Protection.* University of South Carolina, Columbia, 1998.

———, *International Law In the Twenty-First Century.* Rowman & Littlefield, Maryland, 2005.

L de La Fayette, 'Responding to Environmental Damage in Antarctica'. *Antarctica: Legal and Environmental Challenges for the Future.* British Institute of International & Comparative Law, London, 2007.

Lamers, M., Haase, D. & Amelung, B., 'Facing The Elements: Analysing Trends in Antarctic Tourism'. *Tourism Review*, Vol.63, No.1, 2008, pp.15-27.

Maher, P., Steel, G. & McIntosh, A., 'Antarctica: Tourism, Wilderness, and 'Ambassadorship''. USDA Forest Service Proceedings RMRS-P-27. *Seventh World Wilderness Congress Symposium*, 2003.

Mason, Hon. Sir A., 'The International Concept of Equality of Interest in the Sea as it Affects the Conservation of the Environment and Indigenous Interests'. *Land, Rights, Laws: Issues of Native Title.* Vol. 2, Issues Paper No.16, Land Title Research Unit, Australian Institute of Aboriginal and Torres Strait Islander Studies, June 2002, pp.1-6.

Muller, N., 'Alarm Bells Sound for Antarctic Tourist Vessels'. *The Valparaiso Times.* 6 May 2009, Viewed 28 May, 2009, <http://www.valparaisotimes.cl/content/view/524/388/>.

Murray, C. & Jabour, J., 'Independent Expeditions and Antarctic Tourism Policy'. *Polar Record.* Vol. 40, No. 215, 2004, pp.309-317.

Palmer, G., *Environmental Politics: A Greenprint for New Zealand.* John McIndoe, Dunedin, 1990.

Payoyo, P., 'The Common Heritage of Mankind and Global Environmental Governance'. Fourth Annual Common Property Conference. IASCP, Philippines, 1993, pp.1-17.

Scientific Committee on Antarctic Research, *The Antarctic Treaty System: An Introduction.* Viewed 4 May, 2009, <http://www.scar.org/treaty/>.

Scully, R.T. & Kimball, L., 'Antarctica: Is There Life After Minerals?'. *Marine Policy.* April, 1989.

Shackelford, S., 'The Tragedy of the Common Heritage of Mankind'. *Stanford Environmental Law Journal.* Vol. 27, No. 27, 2008, pp.101-157.

Shaw, M., *International Law.* 4th ed., Cambridge University Press, Cambridge, 1997.

Smith, V., 'Foreword'. *People and Tourism in Fragile Environments.* John Wiley & Sons, Chichester, 1996.

———, 'A Sustainable Antarctic: Science and Tourism'. *Annals of Tourist Research.* Vol. 21, No. 2, 1994, pp.221-230.

Suter, K., *Antarctica: Private Property or Public Heritage?*, Pluto Press, Australia, 1991.

Vidas, D., *Emerging Law of the Sea Issues in the Antarctic Maritime Area: A Heritage for the New Century?*, Antarctic Project Report 12/99. The Fridtjof Nansen Institute, Oslo, 1999.

Vigni, P. 'The Secretariat of the Antarctic Treaty: Achievements and Weaknesses Three Years After its Establishment'. *Antarctica: Legal and Environmental Challenges for the Future.* British Institute of International & Comparative Law, London, 2007.

UNESCO, World Heritage Convention: Statistics on States Parties. Viewed October 24, 2009, <http://whc.unesco.org/en/statesparties/stat/#sp3>.

Walton, D., 'Environmental Damage in Antarctica: Measuring the Damage'. *Antarctica in the Environmental Age.* Department of Conservation, Wellington, 1998.

Zovko, I., Vessel-Sourced Pollution in the Southern Ocean'. *Antarctica: Legal and Environmental Challenges for the Future.* British Institute of International & Comparative Law, London, 2007, pp.191-222.

Jane Verbitsky is a Senior Lecturer in the Department of Social Sciences at AUT University in Auckland. Her research interests focus on Antarctica, the security/rights nexus in refugee policy, and justice institutions.

The Role of Human Rights in Environmental Governance: The Challenge of Climate Change

Bridget Lewis

Abstract

The role of human rights in environmental governance is increasingly gaining attention. This is particularly the case in relation to the challenge of climate change, where there is growing recognition of a real threat to human rights. This chapter argues in favour of greater reference to human rights principles in environmental governance. It refers to the experiences of Torres Strait Islanders to demonstrate the impact of climate change on human rights, and the many benefits which can be gained from a greater consideration of human rights norms in the development of strategies to combat climate change. The chapter also argues that a human rights perspective can help address the underlying injustice of climate change: that it is the people who have contributed least to the problem who will bear the heaviest burden of its effects.

Key Words: Human rights law, climate change, Indigenous rights, environmental rights, justice.

*****

1.   Introduction

Climate change is the most significant challenge currently facing the international community. The implementation of effective responses requires that states not only take steps to reduce their own greenhouse gas emissions, but also engage with the wider international community to develop cooperative strategies. A coordinated, cooperative response is necessary for a number of reasons. First, international cooperation recognises the transnational nature of climate change, in that greenhouse gas emissions from one state will cause environmental changes in other states. Flowing from this is the acknowledgment from wealthy states that they will be required to assist poorer states put in place mitigation and adaptation strategies. A cooperative approach also reflects the reality of international relations with regards to climate change: that no state will be prepared to take on the burden for reducing greenhouse gas emissions unless there is a similar commitment from other states.

Environmental governance of climate change must therefore acknowledge the international character of the challenge, and address the disparate liabilities and capabilities of different states, and in particular the inequality between developed and developing states. Human rights principles can help promote and shape this international cooperative approach through their emphasis on equality and non-discrimination, their widespread adoption and applicability to all states, and the set of minimum standards which they provide.

To date research on climate change has tended to come from the fields of science, economics and international relations. The principal research documents on the impacts of climate change are the reports of the Inter-Governmental Panel on Climate Change (IPCC). These reports provide detailed analysis of observed changes in atmospheric greenhouse gases, temperatures, sea levels, precipitation, wind patterns and extreme weather events such as droughts, storms and heatwaves. They provide analysis of the human and natural causes of climate change and model projected future climate change.[1] While the IPCC reports give valuable information about the scientific causes and effects of climate change, they do not directly address the impacts that these effects will have on communities in terms of subsistence and health impacts, loss of traditional lands and ensuing implications for social, cultural and spiritual activities.

Legal scholars have more recently entered the field, searching for legislative or regulatory solutions to climate change, and investigating the way laws enacted in response to climate change might impact on other fields.[2] These legal responses tend to focus on mitigation strategies - mechanisms for reducing the impact of greenhouse gas emissions either through cutting emissions or increasing carbon sinks. Less attention is given in legal frameworks to adaptation strategies - methods for lessening the impact of climate change on human communities by building adaptive capacity, particularly in communities which are more vulnerable to the effects of climate change.

Although legal responses to date have tended to focus on mitigation rather than adaptation, we are starting to see a more widespread acknowledgment of the human impact of climate change,[3] along with a wider acknowledgement that climate change poses a real threat to human rights. The enjoyment of rights such as the right to the highest attainable standard of health, the right to an adequate standard of living, the right to enjoy cultural and traditional customs, even the right to life, are threatened by environmental changes such as rising sea levels, changing temperatures, increased storm activity, or altered migration patterns of animals, birds and fish.

Given the increased recognition of the fact that climate change has implications for the enjoyment of human rights, it is not surprising that there is an emerging debate about what human rights law might require of governments in terms of their responses to climate change. Yet the exact function that human rights law might play in developing legal strategies for climate change adaptation remains largely unexplored. Human rights considerations tend to play a supporting role in discussions about legal responses to climate change. Violations of human rights may be accentuated as part of a call for greater action, but they are rarely constructed as the primary or exclusive justification. Similarly, promotion of human rights may be touted as a positive outcome of a proposed measure, but again this tends to be as a corollary to the principal objectives, which are usually couched in terms of environmental protection, economic development or humanitarian assistance. The entitlements and obligations inherent in human rights law are rarely given a position of prominence in discourse about climate change governance, and relatively little work has been done examining exactly what kind of place human rights law might have in the overall legal or regulatory framework. In a broad sense, climate change raises the question of what role human rights law might play in environmental governance more generally.

This chapter argues that human rights law offers many benefits as a framework upon which to develop responses to the challenge of climate change. It begins by illustrating the links between human rights and the environment generally, outlining existing law which recognises the environmental dimensions of many existing rights and the necessity of a healthy environment as a prerequisite to the enjoyment of human rights. Further, the chapter argues in favour of the development of an independent right to a good environment which would be relevant to environmental governance.

The chapter then considers the specific issue of climate change in more detail, using as a case study the experiences of Torres Strait Islanders to illustrate the impact of climate change on human rights. This example reinforces the suitability of viewing climate change from a human rights perspective. Finally, the chapter outlines some of the benefits which can be gained from taking a human rights approach, both to the specific challenge of climate change, but also to environmental governance more generally. In particular, the chapter argues that a human rights approach can help to instil principles of environmental justice within our response to climate change.

2.   Why Should Human Rights be Involved in Environmental Governance?

The link between the environment and human rights is recognised internationally, both in international law and in instruments of 'soft law'.[4] While debate continues over the existence of 'environmental rights' and what such rights might include, it is acknowledged in international law that the environment plays an important part in securing the enjoyment of human rights. There are several statements in international law which illustrate the environmental dimensions of a range of human rights and position the environment as a prerequisite to the enjoyment of human rights.

In 1972 the United Nations held a Conference on the Human Environment in Stockholm. The outcome of that conference, the *Stockholm Declaration,* was a set of 'common principles to inspire and guide the peoples of the world in the preservation and enhancement of the human environment.'[5] Principle One of the *Stockholm Declaration* recognises that

> '(m)an has the fundamental right to freedom, equality and adequate conditions of life, in an environment of a quality that permits a life of dignity and well-being, and he bears a solemn responsibility to protect and improve the environment for present and future generations. In this respect, policies promoting or perpetuating apartheid, racial segregation, discrimination, colonial and other forms of oppression and foreign domination stand condemned and must be eliminated.'[6]

Twenty years later these principles were further developed at the United Nations Conference on Environment and Development in Rio de Janeiro. The *Rio Declaration* which emerged from that conference, while falling short of expressly acknowledging the links between the environment and human rights, did recognise that all human beings are entitled to a healthy and productive life in harmony with nature.[7] It also enumerates several rights which are to apply in environmental governance. These include the right to information and to participate in decision-making. The Declaration also provides that states should ensure the availability of effective remedies for people affected by environmental degradation.[8] These principles echo human rights norms, such as the right to equal access to justice, the right to participation in government, and the right of access to information. The *Rio Declaration* constructs equity and non-discrimination, two fundamental principles of human rights, as integral elements of the right to sustainable development. This includes the right of future generations to enjoy the benefits of their environment.[9] In this fashion the *Rio Declaration,* although not dealing explicitly with human rights, draws effectively on human rights norms in clarifying the rights and duties of people and states with regards to sustainable development.

The *Draft Declaration on Human Rights and the Environment* of 1994[10] states in its opening principle that 'human rights, an ecologically sound environment, sustainable development and peace are interdependent and indivisible.' It explains that established environmental and human rights principles operate together to guarantee everyone the right to a secure, healthy and ecologically sound environment, and that 'this right and other human rights, including civil, cultural, economic, political and social rights, are universal, interdependent and indivisible.' It also articulates the environmental dimensions of several well-recognised human rights, including the right to life, the right to health and a range of cultural rights.[11]

While statements such as these are prominent in soft law instruments such as the Stockholm and Rio declarations, the link between the environment and human rights has been less well articulated in international human rights treaties. That is not to say, however, that international human rights treaties are silent on the environment. The *Convention on the Rights of the Child*, for example, acknowledges that the provision of clean drinking water is essential to ensuring that all children enjoy the highest attainable standard of health.[12] While key human rights treaties such as the *International Covenant on Civil and Political Rights*[13] and the *International Covenant on Economic, Social and Cultural Rights*[14] do not specifically mention the environment, they do refer to principles such as non-discrimination and equality. As these principles apply to development, they imply an obligation to ensure sustainability and intergenerational equity.

Some regional human rights treaties make stronger statements about the importance of the environment to human rights. The *African Charter on Human and Peoples' Rights*[15] states in Article 24 that all people shall have the right to a generally satisfactory environment which is favourable to their development. The San Salvador Protocol to the *American Convention on Human Rights in the Area of Economic, Social and Cultural Rights*[16] guarantees the right to a healthy environment in Article 11.

Regional human rights organisations have also recognised the role played by the environment. There have been several successful cases in both the Inter-American Court of Human Rights and the European Court of Human Rights which established that environmental degradation in the form of, for example, deforestation or pollution, amounted to a breach of the human rights of communities living nearby, such as the right to health or the right to privacy.[17] These cases confirm that violations of human rights can occur through environmental damage, and explicitly recognise the role the environment plays in ensuring the protection and fulfilment of human rights.

The *Declaration on the Rights of Indigenous Peoples*[18] includes important statements of environmental rights enjoyed by indigenous peoples and individuals. The Preamble to the Declaration recognises that 'respect for indigenous knowledge, cultures and traditional practices contributes to sustainable and equitable development and proper management of the environment.' The Declaration goes on to guarantee to indigenous people several human rights with environmental dimensions, as well as a right to environmental protection, contained in Article 29:

> 'Indigenous peoples have the right to the conservation and
> protection of the environment and the productive capacity
> of their lands or territories and resources. States shall

establish and implement assistance programmes for indigenous peoples for such conservation and protection, without discrimination.'

While the Declaration is not legally binding on states, it is nonetheless an important step in cataloguing the rights of indigenous people and highlights the strong links between environmental protection and human rights.

The significance of environmental protection in promoting the rights of indigenous peoples and individuals is also recognised in other international treaties, such as the International Labour Organisation's *Indigenous and Tribal Peoples Convention*.[19] The Convention requires governments to recognise the special importance of the relationship indigenous peoples have with the environment.[20] It also states that indigenous peoples have the right to participate in decision-making which affects their land and to share wherever possible in the benefits of its exploitation.[21]

The cumulative effect of these statements in international law is to highlight the strong links between the environment and human rights, particularly, the role of human rights principles in defining and promoting sustainable development, and the construction of a good environment as a prerequisite to the enjoyment of a wide range of human rights. These links justify a place for human rights principles in environmental governance. The following discussion examines this proposition with regards to the particular challenge of climate change.

3.   What Rights are Affected by Climate Change?

This chapter considers climate change as a specific kind of environmental degradation, such that the principles relating to human rights and the environment generally are applicable to the specific issue of climate change. The IPCC has predicted that global warming due to greenhouse gas emissions will cause a range of environmental changes, including:

- increased temperatures, leading to ice-cap and glacier melt, with resulting rises in sea-levels and associated coastal flooding;
- changes in rates of rainfall, leading to droughts and floods;
- increased frequency and severity of extreme weather events, such as storms and cyclones;
- shifts in ocean temperatures and currents, with associated impacts on the distribution and migration patterns of marine species;

- increases in prevalence, and shifts in distribution, of mosquito-borne and water-borne diseases, including introduction to new areas.[22]

These physical changes present serious challenges for communities who will experience them. Agriculture, infrastructure, potable water supplies, biodiversity and healthcare are all potentially at risk from the impacts of climate change. To achieve a more detailed understanding of the implications of climate change for communities, particularly indigenous communities, we can look at the case study of the experiences of Torres Strait Islanders.

A. Impact of Climate Change in the Torres Strait

The Torres Strait Islands are a group of over 100 islands located between Cape York Peninsula, the northernmost tip of the state of Queensland in Australia, and Papua New Guinea. The islands are spread over 48,000km², with around 7,100 people living in 18 communities across 16 islands.[23] Each community is a distinct people, with its own traditions, laws, customs and unique history. In spite of this diversity, and despite the fact that the communities are spread out over a very large area, the islands are often grouped together because of their geographic location, and they have developed strong regional links. Torres Strait Islanders have their own flag, which symbolises the unity and identity of all communities in the region. They also have their own regional authority which was created to help Islanders manage their own affairs according to *ailan kastom* (island custom) and develop a stronger economic base for the region.[24]

Climate change is already having a noticeable impact on the islands in the Torres Strait. There is a great deal of anecdotal evidence of impacts such as increased erosion, strong winds and increasing frequency and severity of storms.[25] Many islands have experienced recent incidents of seawater inundation following king tides, with the ocean breaking over sea walls and the foreshore and flooding villages.[26] Salt-water inundation causes widespread damage to infrastructure (roads, airstrips, jetties, and sewerage and drainage systems) and contaminates potable water supplies and arable land. Some communities have been forced to move further inland, or to raise their houses up on stilts to get above the water level when the sea encroaches.[27] Even after the water recedes, the impact on infrastructure, drinking water supplies and agriculture remains.[28] Saltwater inundation also impacts on important cultural and sacred sites, including cemeteries located close to the coast.[29] Changes in ocean temperatures and currents, and erosion of beaches caused by storm activity and strong waves are also impacting on numbers of important totemic species such as dugong and turtles.[30]

Climate change is predicted to cause rises in temperatures, and changes to precipitation patterns. It is expected that rainfall frequency will decrease, but rainfall intensity will increase, causing greater frequency of floods and droughts. Climate change is also anticipated to cause more frequent severe weather events, such as cyclones and tropical storms, bringing storm surges and destructive winds.[31]

Communities in the Torres Strait are particularly vulnerable to these effects of climate change. Not only are many of the islands low-lying, placing them at greater risk of inundation from rising sea-levels, but they are also very remote, giving them limited access to mainland infrastructure, resources and support. Once infrastructure on the islands is damaged, be it through salt-water inundation, storms or flooding, residents may be unable to continue living on the islands. Torres Strait Islanders also rely heavily on their environment for subsistence and economic stability.[32] Fishing is a vital activity both as a source of food and as a commercial enterprise. Changes in ocean temperatures and currents already seem to be impacting on fish stocks in the Torres Strait, with the potential to affect both the Islanders' food supplies and economic stability.[33]

Torres Strait Islanders also have a very special relationship with their environment in terms of the cultural, social and spiritual role that it plays in their lives.[34] This close relationship with the ecosystem that surrounds them puts them at risk of a much wider range of negative impacts from climate change than non-Indigenous Australians. For example, changes in distribution and migration patterns of marine species, because of changes to ocean temperatures and currents, may mean that important totemic species are no longer present. This has an important impact on the cultural and spiritual traditions of island communities. Changes in fish stocks may also cause a decline in traditional fishing practices, with the result that such practices are no longer passed down to younger generations. Traditional medicinal knowledge may also disappear as crucial plant species die out.

Climate change therefore presents a wide range of risks to the Islanders' way of life. This risk is compounded by the position of relative socio-economic disadvantage which Islanders currently endure, which hinders their capacity to adapt effectively to rapid climate change and makes them reliant on assistance from the mainland to cope with the impacts of global warming.[35]

This combination of factors places the Torres Strait Islanders in a position where they may be unable to enjoy their human rights because of the effects that climate change will have on their communities. The next section of the chapter will consider what human rights are at risk from climate change, and illustrate the consequences for Torres Strait Islanders.

B. What Rights are Affected?

From a human rights perspective, climate change presents challenges to the enjoyment of a wide range of rights. In some cases, these rights are already being impacted upon. These are rights which are guaranteed to all people under international human rights law, through their inclusion in United Nations human rights conventions and regional human rights treaties, and also in domestic human rights legislation, such as the *Charter of Human Rights and Responsibilities*[36] of the state of Victoria in Australia, and the United Kingdom's *Human Rights Act*.[37] Through these instruments, governments are under an obligation to take measures to respect, protect and promote human rights. Where climate change places human rights at risk, states are required to implement adequate mitigation and adaptation strategies to ensure their obligations are carried out in good faith.

The *International Covenant on Civil and Political Rights* guarantees to all people the right to life.[38] This is also included in the *Declaration on the Rights of Indigenous Peoples,* which guarantees the right to life, physical and mental integrity, liberty and security of the person.[39] Climate change threatens the right to life not only through changes to food and water supplies and spread of disease, but also more directly from severe storms and flooding. In the Torres Strait lives have already been threatened by king tides and severe storms, and it is predicted that health standards may deteriorate from diminished access to clean drinking water and increased susceptibility to disease.[40]

The *International Covenant on Economic, Social and Cultural Rights* guarantees to all people the right to an adequate standard of living, along with the right to adequate food, clothing and housing, and to the continuous improvement of living conditions.[41] It is predicted that climate change will have a serious impact on food production patterns with changes in rainfall patterns, increased salinity and erosion.[42] Changes to sea levels, ocean temperatures and currents are predicted to cause many fish and marine species to migrate. Torres Strait Islanders rely on fishing as a source of food and an important commercial activity. Islanders have already reported changes in fish stocks, and for these communities, these changes may have a very significant impact on their human rights, affecting their means of subsistence and economic stability.[43]

The *International Covenant on Economic, Social and Cultural Rights* also guarantees the right to the highest attainable standard of health.[44] As mentioned above, the right to health in the Torres Strait is under threat both directly and indirectly from climate change. The right to water has also been specifically recognised as a separate right by the United Nations Committee on Economic, Social and Cultural Rights, because of its importance to rights to health and food.[45] In the Torres Strait, both ground and surface water supplies are at risk of contamination from salt-water incursions. Green explains that many of the islands in the Torres Strait have already exhausted local drinking water supplies, and must rely on mobile or permanent desalination plants to meet demand.[46] The stresses placed on these water supplies by climate change will cause substantial problems for resource management in the Torres Strait, and cause potentially very serious impacts on Islanders' health.[47]

The *Declaration on the Rights of Indigenous Peoples* stresses that Indigenous peoples must equally be able to enjoy the highest attainable standard of health, and further guarantees the right of Indigenous peoples to maintain their traditional medicines and health practices.[48] Climate change is predicted to cause a wide range of negative health impacts, including the spread of diseases into previously unaffected areas, increased prevalence of mosquito and water-borne diseases such as malaria and dengue fever, and aggravation of existing health problems.[49] The impacts on food and fresh water supplies discussed above create a risk of malnutrition and other health problems.

The right to health is already a significant issue for Aboriginal and Torres Strait Islander communities in Australia, who have very poor health statistics, particularly when compared to the quality of health enjoyed by non-Indigenous Australians.[50] This places them at greater risk of adverse health impacts from climate change. The close relationship they have with nature means that environmental degradation has a real impact on their health, in particular their mental health, with the result that climate change may impact on Torres Strait Islanders in ways that do not exist for non-Indigenous Australians.[51] Where traditional medicinal practices involve particular species of flora and fauna, these too may be adversely affected by climate change.

Where the environment plays an important social or cultural role in a community, as it does for Torres Strait Islanders, other rights are under threat from environmental degradation caused by climate change. The ICCPR guarantees the right of all peoples to enjoy their traditional customs, languages and religions.[52] International law recognises a range of rights owed to Indigenous peoples. The International Labour Organisation's *Indigenous and Tribal Peoples Convention* imposes an obligation on states parties to protect Indigenous peoples' social, cultural, religious and spiritual values and practices.[53] It also guarantees to Indigenous people the right to participate in decision-making which affects them, and to set their own priorities for development.[54] The cultural and spiritual significance which Indigenous people give to the land, and their rights to access and control those lands, must also be protected.[55] The *Declaration on the Rights of Indigenous Peoples* also enumerates a range of social, cultural and economic rights to which Indigenous peoples are entitled, including the right to practise and revitalise cultural traditions and customs,[56] the right to practise, develop and teach spiritual and religious traditions, including accessing and maintaining religious and cultural sites,[57] and the right to maintain and practice traditional medicines, including the conservation of medicinal plants, animals and minerals.[58] These rights are at risk where climate change limits a people's ability to carry on their traditional way of life, to pass on traditional customs to younger generations or to remain on their traditional lands. It has been suggested that, in the case of the Torres Strait Islands, the very existence of *ailan kastom* is under threat from climate change.[59]

We can see from the experiences of Torres Strait Islanders that there are a wide range of rights which are under threat from the environmental changes brought about by global warming. We can also clearly see the need for a healthy environment as a prerequisite for the enjoyment of human rights.

4.   The Need to Recognise a 'Right to a Good Environment'

One of the criticisms of a human rights approach to environmental problems like climate change is that it links environmental degradation too closely to human interests, and does not adequately recognise the importance of the environment in its own right. It has been argued that this approach allows some environmental issues to slip through the cracks where they cannot be linked to a particular human rights violation. For climate change, this argument might be seen to have some particular weight, since there will be consequences of climate change that we cannot yet foresee, and identifying the particular human rights impacts which might occur in the future is problematic. If our human rights approach is reliant on identifying a particular individual or group who will suffer a particular breach of human rights before we can take action, then we may find ourselves stymied in our ability to take effective action.

One way of countering this argument, however, would be to recognise a good environment as an independent right, separate from other human rights. Such a right would articulate the fact that all people are entitled to live in a safe and healthy environment. Significantly, to prove a violation of this right it would not be necessary to establish that other human rights have been breached, but rather would require only an objective demonstration of environmental degradation. Acceptance of an independent 'right to a good environment' would recognise the inherent value that the environment has to humanity as a whole. While a separate right to a good environment has not yet been firmly stated in international law, there is growing support for its recognition.[60]

Formulations of a separate right to a good environment can be found in several regional treaties, as outlined above. Similar statements are included in a number of national constitutions as well. More than one hundred constitutions recognise environmental rights in some form or another.[61] In some countries environmental protection has been found to be actionable under the constitution based on other guaranteed rights, such as the right to life. For example, the Indian Constitution guarantees a right to life which has been interpreted by courts as providing a basis for sustainable development and intergenerational equity.[62] Similarly, the Colombian courts have found a basis for an enforceable right to a healthy environment in their constitutional guarantee of the right to life.[63]

In a growing number of countries however environmental protection is enshrined in the constitution in the form of an express right to an environment of a certain quality. For example, the South African Constitution states that

> everyone has a right (a) to an environment that is not harmful to their health or well being; and (b) to have the environment protected, for the benefit of present and future generations, through reasonable legislative and other measures that (i) prevent pollution and ecological degradation; (ii) promote conservation; and (iii) secure ecologically sustainable development and use of natural resources while promoting justifiable economic and social development.[64]

The Constitution of the Philippines provides that 'the state shall protect and advance the right of the people to a balanced and healthful ecology in accord with the rhythm and harmony of nature.'[65] The Constitution of Chile provides a right to live free of contamination. It also places a positive obligation on the Chilean Government to 'ensure that the right to live in an environment free of contamination is not violated' and to 'serve as a guardian for and preserve nature/the environment'.[66] While the Chilean constitution creates a right of action to enforce these protections, many national constitutions which include statements of environmental rights are not justiciable or self-executing. However, as Hill et al have illustrated, these statements still have value as they provide direction for the development of policy and the implementation of legislation.[67] Hiskes outlines several other benefits to be gained from the inclusion of environmental rights within national constitutions. Firstly he points out their importance as a means of trumping legislative provisions, administrative actions, judicial or political decisions which would have the effect of weakening environmental protections. He also points out that having environmental rights enshrined in a constitution allows for a level of coordination across what would otherwise be a 'disparate pastiche' of environmental regulations relating to areas such as air pollution, water quality, dumping and environmental impact statements. This may be particularly pertinent in federal nations such as Australia, where state and territory governments share legislative powers with the Commonwealth government for different areas of environmental protection.[68] Further, it is arguable that the widespread inclusion of these environmental rights in national constitutions may be evidence of emerging state practice which could eventually lead to the recognition of an independent right to a good environment in international law.

5.   Benefits of a Human Rights Approach

A human rights approach to climate change could potentially enable individuals or communities to bring a claim under existing human rights regimes where the actions of a government or corporation have led to environmental damage.[69] Utilising the claims mechanisms provided for by international and regional human rights regimes is one way that human rights law can be used to help achieve redress for peoples adversely affected by climate change, perhaps by providing an avenue to claim compensation, or to achieve justice through holding polluters otherwise accountable. This has already been attempted by Inuit peoples of North America, who brought a petition to the Inter-American Human Rights Commission seeking a declaration confirming that climate change is in fact a human rights issue, and that developed states, and in particular the United States of America, were in breach of their human rights obligations where they have failed to take appropriate steps to mitigate the impact of global warming.[70]

We can also use human rights as a normative framework upon which to build our responses to climate change. If we accept that the protection of human rights is a necessary goal of our climate change strategies, then we can use that objective as a yardstick against which to evaluate policy. Where governments have ratified human rights treaties, they are under a positive obligation to respect, protect and fulfil human rights. This means that at the very least they need to consider the impact on human rights of their policies on climate change, and ensure that they do not make human rights situations worse. Human rights law could be used to lend the weight of international law to criticisms of governments who do not take adequate steps to respond to the threat of climate change.

There are other benefits of taking a human rights approach to climate change. First, it frames the discussion in terms which may have more resonance for the broader community. By focussing on the human impact and on addressing the plight of people who will be affected first (and/or most severely) the debate on climate change can be moved away from the fields of economics, science and diplomacy, which may seem complicated and remote. This is not to suggest that we should abandon these fields of endeavour in favour of a solely human rights-focussed approach. Rather, human rights should be seen as an integral part of our approach, enriching it by offering a new lens through with to view the problem, and offering normative standards against which to evaluate strategies.

One important benefit of a human rights perspective is also one of the imperatives of a human rights-based approach. In taking a human rights focus, it is essential that we involve at-risk communities in consultation and planning, to help identify how their rights are being threatened and particularly to gain an appropriate understanding of the social, religious and cultural implications. There are many benefits to be gained from this approach. For example, it allows us to develop mitigation and adaptation strategies which are formulated with reference to traditional knowledge. In Australia, Aboriginal and Torres Strait Islander peoples have lived through past episodes of climatic change, and have adapted successfully.[71] Traditional knowledge of the natural environment and climatic cycles can be a very valuable resource in developing strategies. Consultation with indigenous communities and allowing for indigenous leadership is also essential if we are to develop strategies which will be culturally appropriate and which will gain the support of communities themselves. [72]

Human rights can also help address the injustice of climate change. Many countries who will suffer worst from the impact of climate change (or at least those who will suffer first) are among the least responsible for its causes. For example, many of the Pacific Islands likely to feel the first impacts of climate change are categorised as Small Island Developing States and are recognised to have contributed a very small proportion of total greenhouse gas emissions when compared to more developed states.[73] Compounding this disproportionate impact is the fact that many of the states in this situation have limited capacity to cope with the environmental damage which they will confront as a result of climate change.

There is another injustice associated with climate change as well. Because of the extended timeframe over which the results of global warming will be played out, there is a generational disparity between the people who have caused the problem and those who will have to live with the consequences. This problem of inter-generational equity is a significant challenge for environmental governance generally. The importance of protecting the environment for the enjoyment of future generations is recognised in both the Stockholm and Rio Declarations. It is no less relevant to the problem of climate change. A human rights perspective requires us to think about the human rights capabilities, not just of our own generation, but of future generations as well. In addition to ensuring that the human rights of present generations are protected, we need to ensure that our actions today will maximise the ability of all people to enjoy their human rights, without jeopardising the chances of future generations of doing the same. Our responses to the challenge of climate change would need to meet this standard.

The recognition of environmental rights in particular offers a chance for us to address the issue of inter-generational equity. By acknowledging the inherent value of the environment to all humanity, we must necessarily accept that it needs to be protected not only for current generations but also so that it can be enjoyed and relied upon by future generations. It has been argued that using human rights as a means to ensure inter-generational justice is problematic because rights are typically constructed as inhering in the individual, and there are difficulties in picturing these individuals in the future in a way which would restrict our behaviour in the present time.[74] It is argued here that the recognition of an independent right to a good environment (as opposed to a construction of environmental protection as a prerequisite to the enjoyment of other established human rights) helps to overcome this argument as it links human rights more closely to sustainable development in a way which necessitates conservation of the environment. Recognition of a specific right to a good environment is therefore closely linked to securing intergenerational equity and can be applied in these terms to the problem of climate change.

The acknowledgement of an independent right would impose upon governments an obligation to take steps to ensure people are able to enjoy a health environment. This would be a significance step beyond the existing rights to information, participation and compensation which apply to environmental matters currently. However, the introduction of a new, independent right to a good environment is not without its obstacles. Some authors have criticised the concept of new right, arguing that it could not be specific enough to be enforceable or that it undermines existing human rights.[75] Others have suggested that a new right is not necessary as existing human rights are adequate.[76] As it has been argued above, a new, independent right to an environment would allow for greater protection of the rights of future generations than is possible relying only on existing human rights. It is suggested that such a right need not be seen to weaken existing human rights protections, but that it could operate alongside existing rights, consistently with the tenets of interdependence and indivisibility.

There is also the challenge of finding a place for the new right within existing international law. Would a new treaty be required? Could the *Declaration on Human Rights and the Environment* form the basis for the negotiation of a new treaty, and if so, what level of support would it have from the international community? It is not denied that these questions are challenging ones, and that a treaty-based independent right to a healthy environment may still be some way off, but the numerous iterations of such a right in national constitutions and in soft-law instruments is evidence of a growing recognition around the world that environmental protection is something to which all individuals and peoples are entitled.

Even without an independent right to a good environment in international law, existing human rights principles ought to still play a significant role environmental governance, and there is much to be gained from their inclusion. By including greater reference to human rights principles in matters that affect the environment, governments acknowledge that environmental degradation has implications for human rights. It is suggested that any assessment of the potential environmental impact of a proposed activity or development ought properly to include reference to potential human rights implications. Further, by acknowledging the important role that the environment plays in promoting the enjoyment of human rights, governments are presented with an opportunity to use environmental protection as a means of fulfilling their human rights obligations.

By recognising the place that human rights law has in the discussion about climate change, we can compile a framework of normative principles, which can guide our approach to mitigation and adaptation. As international law develops, these principles are gaining in strength and enforceability, and will be able to be translated into specific policies and enforceable agreements.[77]

6.   Conclusion

Human rights law has an important role to play in environmental governance generally and in particular in relation to the challenge of climate change. Given the potential of climate change to impact upon the lives of millions of people around the world, in a wide variety of ways, it is an issue of major concern for human rights lawyers. Approaching the issue from a human rights perspective offers many benefits. Not only does it equip us with a normative framework which we can utilise to evaluate and develop responses, but it also helps put the debate about climate change in terms which have more resonance for the wider community, because it forces us to focus on the human impact, rather than the economic or scientific impact, of global warming.

By recognising the threat to human rights which climate change presents we can also hope to address the injustice of climate change. Human rights law forces us to focus on the people who will be most affected. It compels developed nations to make greater efforts towards capacity building in poorer states, in recognition of the fact that developed nations are generally more responsible for global warming. It also compels developing nations to take responsibility for their contribution to climate change and to provide support and assistance to communities most affected by the impacts of global warming. The application of human rights law to the problem of climate change also presents an opportunity to learn from indigenous peoples, who have lived through episodes of dramatic climate change in the past, and to use their experiences and traditional knowledge to inform our responses. The recognition of a right to a good environment which is under threat from climate change would address the injustice which climate change represents towards future generations and the environment generally.

Notes

[1] Intergovernmental Panel on Climate Change, *Climate Change 2007: The Physical Science Basis, Summary for Policy Makers*, Cambridge University Press, Cambridge, 2007.

[2] For example, see F Baker's chapter in this volume, which examines the impact of the UK *Climate Change Act 2008* on the construction industry: F Baker, 'Climate Change Construction & Environmental Accountability', *Environmental Law, Ethics and Governance*, E Techera (ed.), Inter-Disciplinary Press, Oxford, 2010.

[3] For example, United Nations Human Rights Council, *Resolution on Human Rights and Climate Change*, A/HRC/7/23 (28 March 2008); United Nations Human Rights Council, *Resolution on Human Rights and Climate Change*, UN Doc No. A/HRC/10/L.30 (25 March 2009).

[4] The term 'soft law' refers to instruments of a quasi-legal nature which lack the legal force of treaties but which are otherwise instructive in clarifying the scope or content of existing international law, or which may indicate emerging principles with potential to develop into legal norms. The term includes instruments such as declarations, general comments, United Nations General Assembly Resolutions.

[5] *Declaration of the United Nations Conference on the Human Environment*, UN Doc A/CONF.48/14/Rev1 (Stockholm, 16 June 1972) (*Stockholm Declaration*).

[6] *Stockholm Declaration*, art 1.

[7] *Declaration of the United Nations Conference on Environment and Development*, A/CONF 151/26 Vol. 1, principle 11 (Rio de Janeiro, 3-14 June 1992). (Rio Declaration).

[8] Rio Declaration, principle 10.

[9] Rio Declaration, principle 3.

[10] *Draft Declaration of Human Rights and the Environment*, E/CN.4/Sub.2/1994/9, Annex I (1994).

[11] P Sands, *Principles of International Environmental Law* (2nd edn.) Cambridge University Press, Cambridge, 2003, p. 294; M Doelle, 'Climate Change and Human Rights: The Role of International Human Rights in Motivating States to Take Climate Change Seriously', *Macquarie Journal of International and Comparative Environmental Law*, 1 (2004), 179. p 210.

[12] *Convention on the Rights of the Child* (adopted 20 November 1989, entered into force 2 September 1990) 1577 UNTS 3 (CRC) art 24(2) (c).

[13] *International Covenant on Civil and Political Rights* (adopted 16 December 1966, entered into force 23 March 1976) 999 UNTS 171 (ICCPR)

[14] *International Covenant on Economic, Social and Cultural Rights* (adopted 16 December 1966, entered into force 3 January 1976) 993 UNTS 3 (ICESCR)

[15] *African Charter on Human and Peoples' Rights* (adopted 27 June 1981, entered into force 21 October 1986) 21 ILM 58 (1982).

[16] *Additional Protocol to the American Convention on Human Rights in the Area of Economic, Social and Cultural Rights* (adopted 17 November 1988, entered into force 16 November 1999) OAS TS No. 69 (Protocol of San Salvador).

[17] *Lopez-Ostra V Spain*, (1995) Eur Ct H R 38 ; *Mayagna (Sumo) Awas Tingni Community V Nicaragua*, judgement of 31 August 2001, Inter-Am. Ct. H.R. (Ser C) No 79 (2001).

[18] United Nations *Declaration on the Rights of Indigenous Peoples*, UN Doc No. A/RES/61/295, adopted 13 September 2007.

[19] *ILO Convention No 169 Concerning Indigenous and Tribal Peoples in Independent Countries*, opened for signature 27 June 1989, 28 ILM 1382 (entered into force 5 September 1991).

[20] *ILO Convention No 169*, article 13

[21] *ILO Convention No 169*, article 15

[22] Intergovernmental Panel on Climate Change, *Summary for Policy Makers*, 2007.

[23] Australian Bureau of Statistics, *Population Distribution, Aboriginal and Torres Strait Islander Australians 2006,* 4705.0, Viewed on 15 February, 2010, <http://www.abs.gov.au/AUSSTATS/abs@.nsf/DetailsPage/4705.02006?OpenDocument>.

[24] ABC Radio Australia, *Places: Torres Strait Islands*, Viewed on 15 February, 2010, <http://www.abc.net.au/ra/pacific/places/country/torres_strait_islands.htm>; see also the Torres Strait Regional Authority, Viewed on 15 February, 2010, <http://www.tsra.gov.au>.

[25] T Calma, 'Aboriginal and Torres Strait Islander Social Justice Commissioner Native Title Report', Human Rights and Equal Opportunity Commission, 2/2009, 2009, p 231.

[26] United Nations Permanent Forum on Indigenous Issues, *Climate Change: An Overview*, United Nations Department of Economic and Social Affairs, 2007, p. 1.

[27] Da Green, 'How Might Climate Change Affect Island Culture in the Torres Strait?',CSIRO Marine and Atmospheric Research Paper, 011, 2006, p. 1.

[28] E Gerrard, 'Impacts and Opportunities of Climate Change: Indigenous Participation in Environmental Markets', *Land, Rights, Laws: Issues of Native Title: Issues of Native Title,* Issues Paper 13 (2008); Green, 'How Might Climate Change Affect Island Culture in the Torres Strait?', op. cit;

United Nations Permanent Forum on Indigenous Issues, 'International Expert Group Meeting on Indigenous Peoples and Climate Change, Summary Report' E/C.19/2008/CRP.9, 2008.

[29] United Nations Permanent Forum on Indigenous Issues, op. cit.; D Green, 'How Might Climate Change Affect Island Culture in the Torres Strait?' CSIRO Marine and Atmospheric Research, Paper 011, 2006.

[30] Green, 'How Might Climate Change Affect Island Culture in the Torres Strait?' op.cit., p. 4.

[31] Ibid; Intergovernmental Panel on Climate Change (IPCC), 'Climate Change 2007: Synthesis Report Summary for Policymakers' op. cit; Intergovernmental Panel on Climate Change, 'Climate Change 2007: The Physical Science Basis. Summary for Policy Makers', Cambridge University Press, 2007.

[32] Calma, 'Aboriginal and Torres Strait Islander Social Justice Commissioner Native Title Report' loc. cit.

[33] Ibid; Green, 'How Might Climate Change Affect Island Culture in the Torres Strait?' loc. cit.

[34] Green, 'How Might Climate Change Affect Island Culture in the Torres Strait?' loc. cit.

[35] Calma, 'Aboriginal and Torres Strait Islander Social Justice Commissioner Native Title Report' loc. cit.

[36] *Charter of Human Rights and Responsibilities (2006)* Vic

[37] *Human Rights Act 1998* (UK)

[38] ICCPR art 6; Achala Chandani, 'Distributive Justice and Sustainability as a Viable Foundation for the Future of Climate Change', *Carbon and Climate Law Review,* 2, 2007, pp. 152-63.

[39] *Declaration on the Rights of Indigenous Peoples,* adopted by General Assembly Resolution 61/295 on 13 September, 2007, (DRIP) art 7.

[40] Calma, 'Aboriginal and Torres Strait Islander Social Justice Commissioner Native Title Report' loc. cit.

[41] ICESCR, art 11(1).

[42] IPCC, loc. cit..

[43] Calma, 'Aboriginal and Torres Strait Islander Social Justice Commissioner Native Title Report' , loc. cit., p. 239.

[44] ICESCR, art 12.

[45] United Nations Committee on Economic, Social and Cultural Rights, General Comment 15, *The Right to Water*, E/C.12/2002/11, 26 November, 2002.

[46] Green, 'How Might Climate Change Affect Island Culture in the Torres Strait?' loc. cit.

[47] T Calma, 'A Statistical Overview of Aboriginal and Torres Strait Islander peoples in Australia', Viewed on 2 June, 2009, <http://www.hreoc.gov.au/Social_Justice/statistics/index.html#toc41>.

[48] DRIP, art 24.

[49] D Green, 'Climate Change and Health: Impacts on Remote Indigenous Communities in Northern Australia' (CSIRO Marine and Atmospheric Research, Paper 012, 2006) p. 1.

[50] Calma, 'A Statistical Overview of Aboriginal and Torres Strait Islander Peoples in Australia', op. cit.

[51] Calma, 'Aboriginal and Torres Strait Islander Social Justice Commissioner Native Title Report' op. cit; Green, 'Climate Change and Health: Impacts on Remote Indigenous Communities in Northern Australia' op. cit.

[52] ICCPR, art 27; Office of the High Commissioner for Human Rights, General Comment 23, *The Rights of Minorities*, CCPR/C/21/Rev.1/Add.5 (8 April, 1994); CRC art 30; *Convention on the Elimination of All Forms of Discrimination against Women*, (adopted 18 December 1979, entered into force 3 September, 1981) 1249 UNTS 13 (CEDAW) art 15.

[53] *ILO Convention No 169*, art 5.

[54] *ILO Convention No 169*, art 7.

[55] *ILO Convention No 169*, arts 13-15.

[56] DRIP, art 11,

[57] DRIP, art 12.

[58] DRIP, art 24.

[59] Green, 'How Might Climate Change Affect Island Culture in the Torres Strait?' op. cit. p. 4.

[60] Doelle, loc. cit.; S Atapattu, 'The Right to a Healthy Life or the Right to Die Polluted?: The Emergence of a Human Right to a Healthy Environment under International Law', *Tulane Environmental Law Journal*, Vol. 16, 2002, pp. 65-126; D Shelton, 'Human Rights, Environmental Rights, and the Right to Environment', *Stanford Journal of International Law*, Vol. 28, 1991, pp. 103-138; S Turner, 'The Human Right to a Good Environment: The Sword in the Stone', *Non-State Actors and International Law*, Vol. 4, 2004, pp. 277-301; RP Hiskes, 'The Right to a Green Future: Human Rights, Environmentalism and Inter-Generational Justice', *Human Rights Quarterly*, Vol. 27, 2005, pp.1346-1364.

[61] These include the constitutions of Argentina, Bangladesh, Brazil, Chile, Colombia, Costa Rica, Ecuador, Greece, Guatemala, India, Peru, Portugal, the Netherlands, Nigeria, Pakistan, the Philippines, South Africa and Spain. See *Male Declaration on the Human Dimension of Global Climate Change*, adopted 14 November 2007.

[62] B Hill, S Wolfson & N Targ, 'Human Rights and the Environment: A Synopsis and Some Predictions', *Georgetown International Environmental Law Review*, Vol. 16, 2004, 359-402, 383

[63] Constitution of Colombia (1991), article 11

[64] Constitution of the Republic of South Africa (1996), Ch IV, s 24.

[65] Constitution of Philippines (1987), art II s 16

[66] Constitution of the Republic of Chile (1980), art 19.

[67] Hill, Wolfson & Targ, op. cit., p. 381

[68] R Hiskes, *The Human Right to a Green Future: Environmental Rights and Intergenerational Justice,* Cambridge University Press, Cambridge, 2009, p. 132.

[69] Atapattu, loc. cit.; Turner, loc. cit.

[70] M Wagner, 'The Right to Be Cold: Global Warming and Human Rights', *Human Rights 2007: The Year in Review,* Castan Centre for Human Rights, Monash University, Melbourne, 2008, 73-88.

[71] United Nations Permanent Forum on Indigenous Issues, *International Expert Group Meeting on Indigenous Peoples and Climate Change, Summary Report,* loc. cit.

[72] Calma, 'Aboriginal and Torres Strait Islander Social Justice Commissioner Native Title Report' op. cit., pp 252-254.

[73] United Nations Framework Convention on Climate Change Secretariat, *Climate Change: Small Island Developing States*, 2005, p. 2.

[74] Hiskes, 2009, p. 6.

[75] Atapattu, op. cit., pp.110-113; see also P Alston, 'Conjuring Up New Rights: A Proposal for Quality Control', *American Journal of International Law*, Vol. 78 (1984), pp. 607-621.

[76] Atapattu, loc. cit.; Hiskes, loc. cit., 2009.

[77] Calma, 'Aboriginal and Torres Strait Islander Social Justice Commissioner Native Title Report' loc. cit.

Bibliography

Alston, P., 'Conjuring Up New Rights: A Proposal for Quality Control'. *American Journal of International Law*. Vol. 78, 1984, pp. 607-621.

Atapattu, S., 'The Right to a Healthy Life or the Right to Die Polluted?: The Emergence of a Human Right to a Healthy Environment under International Law'. *Tulane Environmental Law Journal*. Vol. 16, 2002, pp. 65-126.

Aisi, R., 'Facing Extinction: Climate Change and the Threat to Pacific Island Countries'. *Reform*. Vol. 90, 2007, pp. 65-67.

Baker, F., 'Climate Change Construction & Environmental Accountability'. *Environmental Law, Ethics and Governance*. E. Techera (ed), Inter-Disciplinary Press, Oxford, 2010.

Barnett, J., 'Adapting to Climate Change in Pacific Island Countries: The Problem of Uncertainty'. *World Development*. Vol. 29(6), 2001, pp. 977-93.

Barnett, J., 'Titanic States? Impacts and Responses to Climate Change in the Pacific Islands'. *Journal of International Affairs*. Vol. 59(1), 2005, pp. 203-19.

Brindal, E., 'Asia-Pacific Justice for Climate Refugees'. *Alternative Law Journal*. Vol. 32(4), 2007, pp. 240-41.

Brown-Weiss, E., 'Climate Change, Intergenerational Equity and International Law'. *Vermont Journal of Environmental Law*. Vol. 9, 2008, p. 615-628.

Calma, T. 'A Statistical Overview of Aboriginal and Torres Strait Islander Peoples in Australia'. 2009. Viewed on 2 June 2009, <http://www.hreoc. gov.au/Social_Justice/statistics/index.html#toc41>.

——, *Aboriginal and Torres Strait Islander Social Justice Commissioner Native Title Report*. Human Rights and Equal Opportunity Commission. 2009.

Chandani, A., 'Distributive Justice and Sustainability as a Viable Foundation for the Future of Climate Change'. *Carbon and Climate Law Review*. Vol. 2, 2007, pp. 152-63.

Constitution of Colombia, 1991.

Constitution of the Philippines, 1987.

Constitution of the Republic of Chile, 1980.

Constitution of the Republic of South Africa, 1996.

Convention on the Elimination of All Forms of Discrimination against Women. Adopted 18, December 1979, Entered into Force, 3 September, 1981, 1249 UNTS 13.

Convention on the Rights of the Child. Adopted 20, November 1989, Entered into Force, 2, September 1990, UNTS Vol 1577.

Doelle, M., 'Climate Change and Human Rights: The Role of International Human Rights in Motivating States to Take Climate Change Seriously'. *Macquarie Journal of International and Comparative Environmental Law.* Vol. 1, 2004, p. 179.

Gerrard, E., *Impacts and Opportunities of Climate Change: Indigenous Participation in Environmental Markets.* Issues of Native Title. Issues Paper 13, 2008.

Green, D., *How Might Climate Change Affect Island Culture in the Torres Strait?* CSIRO Marine and Atmospheric Research Paper 011, 2006.

———, *Climate Change and Health: Impacts on Remote Indigenous Communities in Northern Australia.* CSIRO Marine and Atmospheric Research Paper 012, 2006.

Hill, B., Wolfson, S. & Targ, N, 'Human Rights and the Environment: A Synopsis and Some Predictions'. *Georgetown International Environmental Law Review.* Vol.16, 2004, 359-402.

Hiskes, R.P., 'The Right to a Green Future: Human Rights, Environmentalism and Inter-Generational Justice'. *Human Rights Quarterly.* Vol.27, 2005, pp.1346-1364.

———, *The Human Right to a Green Future: Environmental Rights and Intergenerational Justice.* Cambridge University Press, Cambridge, 2009.

Intergovernmental Panel on Climate Change, *Climate Change 2007: The Physical Science Basis. Summary for Policy Makers.* Cambridge University Press, 2007.

———, *'Climate Change 2007: Synthesis Report Summary for Policymakers.* 2007.

International Covenant on Civil and Political Rights. Adopted 16 December 1966. Entered into Force. 23 March 1976, 999 UNTS 171.

Sands, P., *Principles of International Environmental Law.* 2nd ed., Cambridge University Press, Cambridge, 2003.

Shelton, D. 'Human Rights, Environmental Rights, and the Right to Environment'. *Stanford Journal of International Law.* Vol. 28, 1994, pp. 103.

South Pacific Regional Environment Programme, *Climate Change, Variability and Sea Level Change.* 2009. Viewed on 16 April 2009, <http://www.sprep.org/topic/climate.htm#3>.

Turner, S., 'The Human Right to a Good Environment: The Sword in the Stone'. *Non-State Actors and International Law.* Vol. 4, 2004, pp. 277-301.

United Nations Committee on Economic, Social and Cultural Rights, *General Comment 15: The Right to Water.* UN Doc. No. E/C.12/2002/11, 2002.

United Nations Framework Convention on Climate Change Secretariat, *Climate Change: Small Island Developing States.* 2005.

United Nations General Assembly, *Declaration on the Rights of Indigenous Peoples,* UN Doc. No. A/RES/61/295, adopted 13 September 2007.

United Nations Human Rights Council, *Resolution on Human Rights and Climate Change.* UN Doc. No. A/HRC/7/23, 28 March 2008.

United Nations Office of the High Representative for Least Developed Countries, *Landlocked Developing Countries and Small Island Developing States,* 2009. Viewed on 16 April 2009 <http://www.unohrlls.org/en/sids/44>.

United Nations Permanent Forum on Indigenous Issues, *International Expert Group Meeting on Indigenous Peoples and Climate Change. Summary Report.* UN Doc. No. E/C.19/2008/CRP.9, 2008.

United Nations Permanent Forum on Indigenous Issues, *Climate Change: An Overview.* United Nations Department of Economic and Social Affairs. 2007.

Wagner, M., 'The Right to be Cold: Global Warming and Human Rights'. *Human Rights 2007: The Year in Review.* Castan Centre for Human Rights, Monash University, Melbourne, 2008.

Woodward, A., Hales, S. & Weinstein, P., 'Climate Change and Human Health in the Asia Pacific Region: Who Will be Most Vulnerable?'. *Climate Research*. Vol. 11, 1998, pp. 31-38.

Bridget Lewis is an Associate Lecturer at the Queensland University of Technology, Brisbane, Australia. The author would like to thank Marcelle Burns, Angela Dwyer and Fiona McDonald for their most helpful comments on previous drafts of this chapter.

PART III

Perspectives on Domestic Regulation

Rural Landholders in Queensland, Australia and the Politics of Environmental Law

Jo Kehoe

Abstract
This chapter considers the political context and systems within which environmental laws are made and shaped. What has happened on rural land in Queensland and, more recently to environmental law and policy has been dominated and fashioned by the political cycles, political systems and ideologies of successive governments. Consideration is given to a particularly controversial environmental law: the *Vegetation Management Act 1999* (Qld). This Act, particularly for rural freeholders, engendered the gradual and ever increasing erosion into the traditional sanctity of private land ownership. Much of the angst with statutory regulation for rural landholders has been generated by the politicization of the *Vegetation Management Act 1999* (Qld).The Act is frequently characterised by pre-election promises from the Queensland Labor Party followed by post election changes to the law. Such was the case in the latest Queensland State election in which a particularly controversial and retrospective amendment was brought about by the *Vegetation Management (Regrowth Clearing Moratorium) Act 2009*.

Key Words: Environmental law, vegetation management, rural landholders, retrospective legislation, political systems, politicization of environmental law.

*****

1.   Introduction

Attaining environmental justice continues as a fundamental theme of the conference and this book. Achieving it may include changing the behaviour of an individual or group. This chapter will illustrate that behavioural change for many Queensland rural landholders, which as a particular group is hampered by law making that is neither inclusive nor collective but made in furtherance of pre-election political dealing. The effect of laws on particular groups is similarly considered by Francine Baker who focuses on the impact of climate change legislation in the UK on the property and construction industry and examines the many challenges accompanying increasing regulation. [1] She concludes that communal awareness and collaboration are prerequisites in achieving environmental justice. [2] This chapter will explore the pitfalls and political reality of environmental law making in Queensland which fetter the progression of environmental justice.

The state of Queensland cleared, and continues to clear, more land than the rest of the Australia combined.[3] Inevitably the natural balance of the land has degraded. The detrimental impacts of broad scale land clearing include the loss of biodiversity, destruction of habitat and native species, together with significant impacts on salinity, acidity, and greenhouse gases.[4] Recognition of the degradation of land in Queensland was slow to emerge and even slower to materialize into policy and law. Initial concerns for the land came out of a review of land policy in 1990;[5] but legislation specifically aimed at protecting biodiversity was not introduced until the *Vegetation Management Act 1999* (Qld), (VMA). Paradoxically, the initial effect of this law was devastating on the environment.[6]

The enactment and subsequent amendments of the VMA has done little to engage rural community with the government. The Act was devastating to many rural landholders not least because of the imposition of statutory regulations on formerly unencumbered property rights. For landholders with a freehold title the introduction of the VMA marked the first imposition of legislative controls. Traditionally Australian inheritance of the British political system and the primary sources of both common law and statute have necessarily meant embracing the long-established sanctity of private property.[7] In the past such rights have customarily been reflected and protected in environmental policy and law; more recent times have witnessed the gradual dissolution of those rights as typified by the VMA. Rather than protecting the property interests of private landholders the VMA has challenged and increasingly eroded them.

This chapter will initially explore the historical background of dominant one-party governments within Queensland. Consideration is given to the dramatic collapse of a prolonged conservative period followed by a time of reform when the electoral system changed. The chapter then examines the role of the Green Party, their part in the recent 2009 election and the politicization of the VMA. The chapter then explores the latest 2009 retrospective amendments to the VMA and the impact of these changes on the agricultural community. Finally, consideration is given to the effect of these most recent changes to the legislation on rural landholders in Queensland.

2.   The Historical Context

When Queensland became an independent state and separated from New South Wales in 1859 the overriding ethos was to develop and populate the state. For much of the twentieth century:

> governments in Queensland were battling to maintain the state as a viable entity, administering what was in all important essentials a frontier society and one dependent

entirely on the fruits of primary production for its economic prosperity. The state was underdeveloped and thinly populated, yet covering vast geographical areas. It lacked sufficient capital investment to shield the economy from the ill effects of droughts, floods and rural recessions.[8]

The overriding drive to develop and clear land, coupled with white settler yeomanry, fostered land polices and agricultural practices which were ultimately difficult to reconcile in a harsh and variable Australian climate.[9]

For Queensland, the management of land, and more recently environmental law and policy, has been dominated and fashioned by the political cycles, political systems and ideologies of successive governments. There is a long established tradition within Queensland of a dominant political party holding office for an extensive period. Thus the longest serving National or conservative party premier, Johannes Bjelke-Petersen, held office for almost twenty years from 1968 to 1987. Throughout this period the power of the agricultural lobby was at its height; and, as premier, Bjelke-Petersen was obliged to leave his own broadscale land clearing business to meet the demands of parliamentary life. Rural landholders, particularly freeholders, enjoyed unfettered rights of ownership and engaged with an empathetic government. This particular conservative period, which ended with the demise of Bjelke-Petersen and subsequently the National Party, lasted for thirty-two years.[10]

The downfall of the Bjelke-Petersen administration followed an independent inquiry, undertaken by Tony Fitzgerald, which found evidence of entrenched and widespread corruption within Queensland.[11] The Inquiry began in May 1987 and lasted until June 1989, at which time it was concluded a great deal remained to be done within the state. Charges against Bjelke-Petersen for official corruption and perjury during the inquiry were ultimately withdrawn following a trial and a hung jury. Clearly a great deal did remain to be done: the jury foreman at the trial was a branch secretary of Bjelke-Petersen's political party.[12] Nevertheless, this period was described as a time of hope for Queensland '...as it began the Herculean task of cleaning its Augean stables.'[13]

3.   Reform of the Electoral System - Optional Preferential Voting

One essential task was reform of the electoral system. The longevity of the Bjelke-Petersen era owed much to the electoral system prevailing at that time. A prime area of concern for the Fitzgerald Inquiry was the issue of fairness of the electoral process, particularly electoral laws, zones and boundaries, which were challenged as biased in favour of the Bjelke-Petersen Government.[14] The challenges primarily concerned the unfair advantage given by both electoral gerrymander and malapportionment.[15] One of the major recommendations of the Inquiry therefore was the formation of an independent Electoral and Administrative Review Commission charged with undertaking an extensive review of electoral and administrative processes.[16]

Following this wide-ranging review, in which submissions were made and public hearings held, the Electoral and Administrative Review Commission recommended electoral reform. The controversial issues of electoral boundaries and zones were to be addressed by independent bodies 'free from interference by the government of the day.'[17] Change in the voting system was also recommended: from compulsory preferential voting to optional preferential voting. In keeping with legislation of that period the *Electoral Act 1992* (Qld), which facilitated many of the changes, did not include an object or purpose clause but, following the Fitzgerald recommendations, it established an independent Electoral Commission and more equitable electoral districts and redistributions.[18]

As a voting system, optional preferential voting is described by the Electoral Commission as 'an unusual, if not unique, voting system.'[19] The shift to this system marked the fourth change to voting methods in the state. Prior to this Queensland had adopted full preferential voting, the more common voting method used within Australia. Queensland and the New South Wales Lower House are the only states to use optional preferential voting. Optional is perhaps a misleading term in that voting in Australia is compulsory. In this context the term means that voters have the option to vote for one candidate only or to vote for one candidate and allocate preference to some or all of the other candidates. The winning candidate needs to secure an absolute majority of the votes cast. If this is not achieved on the first count the candidate with the fewest votes is eliminated and their preferences are allocated. This process continues until one candidate has a majority of votes. In contrast, compulsory preferential voting requires the voter to allocate preference to all candidates.[20]

The post-Fitzgerald reforms were primarily driven by the Queensland branch of Australian Labour Party (ALP) and their leader at the time Wayne Goss. Despite concerns from all parties as to the desirability of adopting optional preferential voting the influence of the Fitzgerald Inquiry pervaded and the *Electoral Act 1999* (Qld) was unopposed in parliament.[21] For the first time in Queensland, changes were made to the voting system not simply because of 'perceived benefit by the government of the day.'[22] In 1989, the year the Fitzgerald Inquiry handed down its report, Queensland Labour won over 50% of the votes cast in the state election as the inevitable electoral backlash against the former Bjelke–Petersen administration took its toll.[23] The end of this politically conservative and evidently dark period meant that Labour returned to dominate the political arena and have generally done so, apart from a two-year interlude, from 1989 to the present.[24]

The optional preferential voting system has continued to date. In the first three elections following the changed voting system the effects were marginal.[25] Indeed it appeared that the 'Electoral Commission of Queensland, quietly 'disapproved' of optional preferential voting - and certainly did not actively promote the concept'[26] in those initial three elections. Over time, as the incumbent government, the ALP have predictably adopted a tactical use of this voting system; and, starting in the 2001 election, campaigned voters to vote just for the ALP, a strategy known as 'plumping' which effectively turns the election into a first past the post race.[27] The outcome of an election with a high rate of plumping is that a candidate may be elected with less than a clear majority of votes. The Queensland voting system therefore appears to perpetuate a dominant single party government and renders representation for minor parties, such as the Greens, a remote possibility.

For Queensland a very real concern is that 'the optional preferential system produces a less representative and less democratic outcome than the compulsory preferential system.'[28] It is only under the latter system that 'elected representatives could genuinely claim to represent the electorate.'[29] The irony is that this voting system was established in an apparently genuine bi-partisan attempt to adhere to the recommendations of the Fitzgerald Inquiry. Back in 1989 the Inquiry noted: 'It is no solution to the deep-seated problems which have occurred to simply replace one set of imposed ideas and approaches to administration with another.'[30]

More recently, Tony Fitzgerald addressed an audience in the State Library of Queensland gathered to commemorate the twentieth anniversary of the Fitzgerald Report. Of current politics in Queensland he had this to say:

> Access can now be purchased, patronage is dispensed, mates and supporters are appointed and retired politicians exploit their connections to obtain 'success fees' for deals between business and government. Neither side of politics is interested in these issues except for short-term political advantage as each enjoys or plots impatiently for its turn at the privileges and opportunities which accompany power.[31]

Subsequently in Parliament, Anna Bligh the Queensland Premier, addressed the issue of accountability in government; and noted some of the reforms her government has made for example in such areas as the freedom of information.[32] She failed to mention her government's tendency to put to Cabinet documents which the government wishes to stifle. This is a tactic which ensures that such documents are not subject to freedom of information requirements for thirty years and was employed by the Queensland Labour Party on the introduction of the VMA in order to suppress a report by the

Department of Primary Industries on the economic impact of vegetation management legislation on rural landholders.[33]

4.   The Role of the Greens in Queensland

The Greens first appeared upon the Queensland election scene in the 1995 election when they contested 28 seats and polled 2.87% of the vote.[34] This voting percentage was reasonably consistent for the following two elections and increased to 6.76% in the 2004 election and 8.37% in the latest 2009 election.[35] This increase has been attributed to the 'substantial interstate migration to the state's southeast, a pattern that has contributed to a partial transformation of Queensland's traditional political culture to one more disposed to Green support.'[36] The Greens remain however, a minor party and such support translates for Queensland Labour into the electoral benefits of Green preference deals, particularly in marginal seats.[37] The influence of the Greens cannot therefore be underestimated because it is in those marginal seats, particularly in the southeast corner of the state, that an election may be won or lost.

The electoral impact of the Green Party within Queensland has been chequered. Essentially state elections, particularly the 2009 election, are a contest between the two main parties being the ALP and the recently formed conservative LNP (Liberal National Party).The degree to which the Green party allocates preferences and stands beneath the 'Labour umbrella' appears to vary with each Queensland election.[38] It is apparent in the most recent 2009 election. As a minority party preference deals for the Greens appear to be their only realistic chance of making an impact. In the 2009 election Green preferences were directed towards the ALP in 14 marginal seats.[39] For the ALP two electoral districts were particularly reliant on Green preference support: they were the Barron River and Everton. In the Barron River district on first preference votes the LNP polled 43.83% compared to the ALP's 43.2%.[40] Three candidates contested this seat and, since the first preference votes fell short of a majority, the Green's contender was excluded and her preferences distributed to the ALP who was boosted to 52% of the total vote and the winning seat.[41] A similar picture emerged in Everton when, following counting on first preference votes the ALP had 44.39% and the LNP 44.12%.[42] Once again the Green preferences enabled the ALP to secure 51% of the vote and the winning seat.[43]

Within the Queensland Parliament, the Green Party had a Member of Parliament sit for a short period by default. In October 2008 Ronan Lee the ALP member for Indooroopilly defected to the Greens. He was defeated by the LNP in the latest 2009 election. Accordingly, in the absence of parliamentary representation, Green preference deals of varying degrees appear set to continue. Part of the payback for such deals comes in the form of controversial environmental laws such as the most recent amendments to the VMA.

5.   The Vegetation Management Act 1999 (Qld)

The politicization of the VMA has a far-reaching potential to disengage the rural community and this is particularly so following the latest election. The Queensland Labor government returned to power for their fifth consecutive term in 2009. Under the optional preferential voting system Labor gained 51 seats with 42.25% of the vote, the LNP took 38 seats with 41.60% of the vote; and the Green Party, with 8.37% of the vote, were unable to secure any seats.[44] The Greens appear to have prompted the latest changes to the VMA even if not to the extent desired. Prior to this most recent election the Green's biodiversity and environment policy on vegetation was described as being to amend the VMA 'to protect endangered, of concern and high conservation value regrowth vegetation, all remnant vegetation in urban areas, and vegetation in riparian and wildlife corridors.'[45] As part of her election campaign Labor Premier Anna Bligh suggested her government may introduce a moratorium on clearing regrowth vegetation.

Queensland Labor were duly re-elected and returned to govern on 21 March 2009. The regrowth moratorium was announced in a ministerial release on the 7 April. It was to take effect from midnight of the same day. The ban on clearing covered endangered regrowth vegetation and the Minister for Natural Resources Mines and Energy, Stephen Robertson, instructed the regulator's 'compliance officers to actively monitor and investigate compliance with the moratorium.'[46] On the 7 April the Labor Government thus announced a retrospective moratorium: this was a law yet to be made. Indeed the opening of the Queensland Parliament did not take place until the 21 April. The first parliamentary session was held on the 22 April at which time the *Vegetation Management (Regrowth Clearing Moratorium) Bill 2009* was introduced. The Act is now deemed to have started on the 8 April.[47]

6.   Retrospective Legislation and a Unique Parliamentary System

Parliaments within Australia have a general power to make retrospective legislation but are presumed to do so prospectively. There is a long held presumption against retrospective laws: against making actions which were formally lawful, unlawful.[48] The Queensland Government's legislative statutory standards are provided for in the *Legislative Standards Act 1992* (Qld), they require that new laws are 'consistent with the principles of natural justice' and 'do not adversely affect rights and liberties, or impose obligations, retrospectively.'[49]

Legislation has a relatively unfettered route within the Queensland parliamentary system. Being a unicameral system it is unique amongst

Australian states. The ALP abolished the Upper House in 1922. The effect of this, as shown by the VMA, is that a majority government may railroad through statutory reform without any heed to divergent interests either within or beyond the confines of the Lower House or Legislative Assembly. In the absence of an Upper House, a means of reviewing legislation in the Queensland parliamentary process falls upon the Scrutiny of Legislation Committee (SLC). The purpose, inter alia, of the SLC is to consider the application of fundamental legislative principles,[50] which are defined as those principles that 'underlie a parliamentary democracy based on the rule of law.'[51] Fundamental legislative principles however were not considered by the SLC in this instance because the *Vegetation Management (Regrowth Clearing Moratorium) Bill 2009* was dealt with as an urgent Bill and once the Bill became an Act, and therefore a law, the responsibility of the SLC ended.[52]

How then did the Queensland Government explain the retrospective moratorium? The Explanatory Notes which customarily accompany a new statute acknowledge that the retrospective application of the Act 'arguably offends' the government's own legislative standards legislation.[53] The defence being that: 'the Premier made an election commitment on the 15 March 2009 to a three month moratorium on endangered regrowth vegetation while consultation with stakeholders occurred to improve vegetation management laws'.[54] The retrospective moratorium was further explained as necessary to prevent pre-emptive clearing and 'justified where the interest of the public as a whole outweigh the interests of an individual'.[55]

To pass the retrospective moratorium, parliamentary debate was declared urgent. The Labour Government utilised a standing order, suspended normal parliamentary business and debated the legislation in one day's sitting.[56] It was noted by the ALP Leader of the House that the urgency was necessary 'to protect the forests of Queensland'.[57] It was noted by opposition and independent members that the urgency was necessary to appease the Green Party for pre-election preference deals.[58]

7.   The Impact of Retrospective Legislation on Rural Landholders

For rural landholders there was opportunity to make submissions on the Act to the relevant regulators and their own Members of Parliament. In the past consultations surrounding amendments to the VMA have been initiated and subsequently disregarded by Queensland Labour.[59] Once again a law promising certainty has generated yet more confusion. Regrowth vegetation affected by the moratorium is coloured blue on the mapping system adopted by the regulators. The areas coloured blue currently include pastures, crops and part of the township of Dalby.[60] Rights of appeal on moratorium maps are suspended for the duration of the moratorium which was set to last for three months and subsequently extended for an additional three months as provided for in the legislation.[61] The moratorium thus lasted for six months until the 7th October 2009 and the effect on one particular landholder from Mitchell was described:

> With the introduction of the Moratorium Bill we expect that our overall production will fall by as much as a quarter in the next 6 years, reducing our property's value to approximately 50%. As responsible land managers we value trees as an essential part of a balanced ecosystem, particularly when used in order to create shade, wildlife corridors and wind breaks. We also use trees such as Brigalow for soil conditioning, as they have the unique ability to place nitrogen back into the soil. However there is a major difference between well managed, ecologically healthy stands of Brigalow, that contribute greatly to soil and plant health, and Regrowth Brigalow, which creates a thick monoculture, causing reduced wildlife numbers and erosion due to lack of ground cover. We have planned for a future on the land, and invested 100% of what we have to give, both financially and physically. We hope that one day our children will want to take on our 'sustainable and profitable' business that provides an irreplaceable resource for Australia and the world.[62]

And from a landholder in Goondiwindi:

> Our family-run property is located near Westmar, on the southern boundary of Dalby Regional Council. Our family has owned and run this property for 35 years, we are a third generation cropping and cattle property, with all three generations living and working for our current and future livelihood. Already due to legislation, we have a third of our property that we cannot touch as it is timbered. The area that you are proposing on the moratorium is partly made up of shade lines and wind breaks that we have purposefully left, so it seems we have been penalized for doing the right thing.[63]

One Member of Parliament tabled letters received from rural landholders, for example:

> We are very angered by this latest attack on the farming sector by the Labor government. This latest attack is

nothing more than a grab for green votes so as to secure another term in office. There is no economic, ecological or environmental reason for this latest land grab from the current government. Mrs Bligh doesn't give a toss about endangered regrowth, the Great Barrier Reef or the welfare of country Queensland—all this is a grab for power at farmer's expense and an agenda from the extreme greens to stop land clearing altogether.

As a business sector we felt that we had managed the current land clearing (vegetation management legislation) well and had adjusted our economics and land management practices accordingly. We have been dealt another severe blow to our industry and cannot trust a government that keeps changing the goal posts and the laws to suit. Furthermore the mapping that we have been issued that covers the latest land grab (blue spots on the maps) are incorrect. Areas shown on our maps that are now to be locked up with no further regrowth management are predominantly grass pastures. Other farmers have said that their blue dots cover the sorghum crop perfectly. The mapping that this land grab is based on is also incorrect.[64]

One continuing area of contention between rural landholders and the vegetation management regulations has been on the issue of clearing mulga. The regrowth moratorium has once again made this type of clearing problematic. During periods of drought mulga is an essential feed-stock for cattle. Queensland has recently endured a prolonged and, in some areas, unprecedented drought. A landholder from Dirranbandi stresses the importance of mulga and the implications of not being able to clear it for feed-stock:

...there are several patches of moratorium blue on our map including the regrowth mulga which has deliberately been regrown by us to use for fodder harvesting should we have another drought, which is inevitable, just a matter of when. Our situation is that we are prepared to keep the mulga for however long we can but we need to be able to use it when we have to (instead of selling our very precious breeding herd again). The stands of mulga are never completely 'wiped out' as it is too valuable to us.[65]

The impact of the moratorium also affected rural land sales. A real estate agent specializing in the marketing of rural properties in the Roma distract had this to say:

> I have attached details on a property we had recently marketed for Auction. However due to the introduction of the Moratorium and the dramatic effects it had on this particular property we had to cancel the Auction in the last few days prior to Auction as all interested parties withdrew their interest ... The Vendors had spent a considerable amount of money on advertising (in excess of $12,000) and I had also invested considerable time and money in conducting several inspections on the property (250km round trip just to conduct the inspection).The Vendors had only purchased the property 18 months earlier for $6M and it was expected that a similar figure would have been achieved at our scheduled Auction. As all interest in the property was withdrawn following the implementation of the Moratorium it can be assumed that this action by your government has resulted in the loss of commission income to this business in excess of $100k, a loss in Transfer Stamp Duty to your own Government of approx $200k and an even greater figure, yet to be determined, in a capital loss to the Owners of the property. Contrary to Mr Stephen Robertson's comments that this Moratorium will not result in the loss of any jobs, this as you can see is already having a negative impact in our business which will impact not only immediately but also on future business sustainability.[66]

A potential issue therefore for rural landholders is that of compensation. The *Legislative Standards Act 1992* (Qld) requires fair compensation for the compulsory acquisition of property.[67] The 2009 amending VMA legislation stipulates that no compensation will be payable under the moratorium as this is an interim measure and a means of exploring 'longer term options'.[68] The VMA was initially passed in 1999 but it took the Labour Government until the contentious 2004 amendments to make a financial commitment to landholders affected by the legislation. Much of the earlier reticence on the part of the Queensland Government was attributed to the unwillingness of the Commonwealth Coalition Government to contribute to a financial assurance for affected landholders. With the latest amendments the government has stated their regulators 'will investigate the costs of any future regulation including potential cost to enterprises made unviable'.[69] The

Queensland ALP has yet to declare if any financial contribution will be expected or forthcoming from the Commonwealth ALP.

8.   Rural Landholders and the Queensland Government

The political sensors of Queensland Labour in the 2009 state election may well have been attuned to the immediate requirements of an election; but there remain matters of critical importance to the environment for which cooperation with the rural community will be essential - for example emissions trading schemes. The government cannot ignore the rural community. In Queensland 141.4 million hectares is devoted to agriculture.[70] Much of the agricultural activity in the state is centred on livestock grazing with relatively small pockets currently under nature conservation or managed resource protection.[71] In economic terms the total value of Queensland's primary industry commodities for 2008 to 2009 is just over $13 billion with cattle being one of the highest value industries.[72] It is crucial for the environment that the Labour Government works with the rural community. It is clear this may be a problematic journey.

One difficulty for the government will be to establish credibility when the gulf between political rhetoric and political practice is so wide. It is imperative for all major parties to embrace environmental issues: the environment is a key electoral influence. Prior to the 2009 election a survey of attitudes of Queensland voters towards land clearing and the environment was undertaken on behalf of the World Wildlife Fund.[73] Almost three quarters of Queensland voters polled said that the environment would have a strong influence on their vote.[74] How then does the Labour Government measure up environmentally? Is there any parity between what is said and what is done?

The VMA brought an end to broadscale land clearing in Queensland in 2006.The long term environmental significance of this legislation cannot be under estimated.[75] The politicization of the VMA has however engendered alienation in the rural community. This estrangement is exacerbated by the government's support of the recent surge in mining and mineral exploration permits on rural land. A total of $563.3 million was invested in exploration permits between 2007 and 2008; this amount is double the previously assessed period.[76] In February 2009 the government amended the *Acquisition of Land Act 1967* (Qld) for those affected by land resumption. The potential advance of mining on prime agricultural land has caused alarm and anguish in the bush.[77] Not least because clearing for mining is not regulated under the VMA.[78]

Similar issues have recently emerged for nature refuges within the state. A relatively small proportion of land is currently conserved under this type of voluntary agreement made between landholders and the government.[79] In Queensland, provision is made for such agreements under the *Nature Conservation Act 1992* (Qld). The object of the Act is the conservation of nature and the emphasis is on community participation.[80] Yet a growing number of nature refuges have been subjected to mining and mineral exploration. The 8000 hectare Bimblebox Refuge in Central Queensland is currently under a very imminent mining threat from Waratah Coal Company.[81] The significant cultural and natural resources and values of Bimblebox are listed to include 'a large area of intact habitat in a landscape that has been subjected to widespread clearing'.[82] A similar fate awaits the Avocet Nature Refuge which supports 'vegetation ecosystems considered endangered in the brigalow belt bioregion'.[83] The Premier of the Labour Government has said exploration permits on nature refuges will be considered on a case by case basis. A genuine acknowledgement of the environmental significance of these sanctuaries should impose a blanket ban on such exploration.

9.   Conclusion

Ideally the environment should be beyond political expediency. The reality for Queensland however is that minority groups may from time to time find themselves in a position to influence and shape government environmental policy and law. The result, as demonstrated by the VMA, generates a lack of attention by a dominant majority government to basic legislative and scrutiny roles. A further outcome is the marginalisation of the rural landholders as those most affected by the VMA. In the past the rural community in Queensland had an influential role within the state. More recently this has lessened to the status of a marginalised group struggling to find a voice and a genuine participatory place in policy decision making affecting rural land. Queensland may have moved on from the Fitzgerald Inquiry era, nonetheless it is crucial to constantly review our parliamentary systems and political processes and question the degree to which they are truly representative and meet the needs of wider society.

Notes

[1] F Baker, 'Climate Change Construction & Environmental Accountability', *Environmental Law, Ethics and Governance*, E. Techera (ed.), Inter-Disciplinary Press, Oxford, 2010.
[2] ibid.
[3] The Australia Institute, 'Land-Use Change and Australia's Kyoto Target', Submission to Senate Environment References Committee Inquiry into Australia's Response to Global Warming, (1999). Auspoll research report prepared for the World Wildlife Fund, *Attitudes towards Land Clearing and Environmental Issues in Queensland, (2009)*.

[4] Australian Conservation Foundation, 'Land clearing in Queensland: the problem and the solution'; AK Krockenberger, RL Kitching & SM Turton, 'Environmental Crisis: Climate Change and Terrestrial Biodiversity in Queensland,' Cooperative Research Centre for Tropical Rainforest Ecology and Management, Rainforest CRC, Cairns, 2003; H Cogger et al., report prepared for the World Wildlife Fund, 'Impacts of Land Clearing on Australian Wildlife in Queensland', 2003, in which clearing rates between 1997 and 1999 were used to calculate that approximately 100 million native mammals, birds and reptiles have died each year as a result of broadscale clearing of remnant vegetation: Viewed on 4 June 2009, <http://wwf.org.au/publications/qld_landclearing/>.

[5] PM Wolfe, DG Murphy & RG Wright, *Report of a review of Land Policy and Administration in Queensland,* Land Policy and Administration Review Committee, Queensland, 1990.

[6] J Kehoe, 'Environmental Law-Making in Queensland: The Vegetation Management Act 1999, (Qld)', *Environmental and Planning Law Journal,* Vol 26, 2009 p. 399.

[7] See G Bates, *Environmental Law in Australia,* 6th edn., Butterworths, Sydney, 2006, pp.20-21.

[8] D Murphy, R Joyce & M Cribb (eds), *The Premiers of Queensland,* University of Queensland Press, Queensland, 1990.

[9] See Bates, op.cit. Ch14.; N Gunningham & P Grabosky (eds), *Smart Regulation Designing Environmental Policy,* Clarendon Press, Oxford, 1998, chapter 5.

[10] Queensland Parliament, Precis of Results of Queensland State Elections 1932 to 2006, viewed 4 June 2009, <http://www.parliament.qld.gov.au/view/historical/electionsReferendums.asp?SubArea=electionsReferendums_electionDates>.

[11] GE Fitzgerald, *Report of a Commission of Inquiry Pursuant to Orders in Council,* Queensland Government Printer, Brisbane, 1989, Viewed 4 June 2009, <http://www.cmc.qld.gov.au/data/portal/00000005/content/81350001131406907822.pdf>. This Inquiry was announced by the acting premier at the time, Bill Gunn, whilst Bjelke-Petersen was overseas, the announcement followed the catalytic ABC Four Corners investigative Report, 'The Moonlight State', 1987, which highlighted the systemic corruption within both the Queensland government and police.

[12] R Fitzgerald, L Megarrity & D Symons, *Made in Queensland, A New History,* University of Queensland Press, 2009, p.185.

[13] R Evans, *A History of Queensland,* Cambridge University Press, Cambridge, 2007, p.249.

[14] G E Fitzgerald, op.cit., p127.

[15] Electoral and Administrative Review Commission, *Report on Queensland Legislative Assembly Electoral System, Volume 1- The Report,* November 1990, defines gerrymander as drawing electoral boundaries to enhance the likelihood of election; and malapportionment as a term used to describe the existence of electoral districts which have significant difference in the number of electors, p.xiii.

[16] GE Fitzgerald, op.cit., pp.370-371.

[17] Electoral and Administrative Review Commission, op.cit., p. 232.

[18] *Electoral Act 1992* (Qld).

[19] Queensland Electoral Commission, Optional Preferential Voting, Fact Sheet, Viewed 4 June 2009, <http://www.ecq.qld.gov.au/asp/index?pgid =170>.

[20] Submissions of arguments both for and against each voting system are detailed in: Electoral and Administrative Review Commission, chapter 6.

[21] Electoral and Administrative Review Commission, pp. 55-56; and Queensland , Legislative Assembly, Electoral Bill, Second Reading, pp5242 - 5251 and pp.5253 -5291.

[22] J Wanna, 'Democratic and Electoral Shifts in Queensland: Back to First Past the Post Voting,' Governance and Public Policy Research Centre, Griffith University, Brisbane, 2004.

[23] Queensland Government, Comparison of Party Performance Queensland State Elections 1977-2001, Table 2B.The percentage of votes for the National Party fell from 40% in the 1986 election to 24% in 1989. Viewed 4 June 2009, <http://www.parliament.qld.gov.au/view/historical/documents/electio ns Referendums/PartyPerformanceStateElections.pdf>.

[24] ibid

[25] Wanna, op.cit., p.2.

[26] ibid, p.2.

[27] This was especially the case with the 2001 Queensland state election, see for example: S Stockwell, 'The Impact of Optional Preferential Voting on the 2001 Queensland State Election,' *Queensland Review*, Vol. 10, no.1, May 2003, pp. 155-162. The Electoral and Administrative Review Commission, *Report on Queensland Legislative Assembly Electoral System, Volume 1: The Report,* November 1990, defines first past the post voting as a system where the winning candidate is the one who receives the largest number of votes regardless of whether a majority is obtained. This system is used in the UK, USA, Canada and New Zealand and was for a period, from 1860 to 1892, adopted in Queensland.

[28] Stockwell, op.cit., p. 155.

[29] Wanna, op.cit., p.2.

[30] GE Fitzgerald , op.cit., p.357.

[31] GE Fitzgerald, The Tony Fitzgerald Lecture, 28 July 2009, Viewed 30 October 2009, <http://www.griffith.edu.au/arts-languages-criminology/key-centre-ethics-law-justice-governance/news-events/tony-fitzgerald-lecture-series-and-scholarship-fund>.

[32] Queensland, Legislative Assembly, Ministerial Statements, Agriculture Industry, per Hon AM Bligh, p. 1904, 1 September 2009. Viewed 30 October 2009, <http://parlinfo.parliament.qld.gov.au/search/>.

[33] s36 (1) (a) *Freedom of Information 1992* (Qld). See also J Kehoe, 'Environmental Law-Making in Queensland: The Vegetation Management Act 1999,' *Environmental and Planning Law Journal*, Vol. 26, 2009, p. 401.

[34] Queensland Government, Comparison of Party Performance Queensland State Elections 1977-2001, Table 2B and 2A, Viewed 4 June 2009, <http://www.parliament.qld.gov.au/view/historical/documents/electionsRefer endums/PartyPerformanceStateElections.pdf>.

[35] Queensland Government, Total Formal First Preference Vote by Party, 2009 State Election, Viewed 4 June 2009, <http://www.ecq.qld.gov.au/>.

[36] PD Williams, 'The Greening of the Queensland Electorate?' *Australian Journal of Political Science*, Vol.41, no.3, Sept 2006, pp. 325-337.

[37] Williams, ibid, p.329 considers the arguments for and against preference allocation.

[38] D Hutton, 'The Greens and Electoral Politics', *Arena Magazine*, Fitzroy, Vic, No.22, Apr/ May 1996, pp. 14-16.

[39] Personal Communication with Drew Hutton from the Queensland Green Party on 29 June 2009.

[40] Electoral Commission Queensland, Barron River, District Summary, Viewed 9th September 2009, <http://www.ecq.qld.gov.au/elections/state/state2009/results/district5.html>.

[41] Electoral Commission Queensland, Barron River, Booth Details, Summary of Distribution of Preferences, Viewed 9th September 2009, <http://www.ecq.qld.gov.au/elections/state/state2009/results/district5.html>.

[42] Electoral Commission Queensland, Everton, District Summary, Viewed 9th September 2009, <http://www.ecq.qld.gov.au/elections/state/state2009/resu lts/district28.html>.

[43] Electoral Commission Queensland, Everton, Booth Details, Summary of Distribution of Preferences, Viewed 9th September 2009, <http://www. ecq.qld.gov.au/elections/state/state2009/results/booth28.html>.

[44] Queensland Electoral Commission, 2009 State General Election, Viewed 4 June 2009, <http://www.ecq.qld.gov.au/elections/state/state2009/results /summary.html#13>.

[45] The Greens, Queensland State Election, Biodiversity and Environment Policy para 12, Viewed 4 June 2009, <http://qld.greens.org.au/election/policy/biodiversity-and-environment>.

[46] S Robertson, '1,000,000 Hectares of Critical Regrowth under Moratorium', Media Release 7 April 2009, Viewed 4 June 2009, <http://www.statements.cabinet.qld.gov.au>.

[47] *Vegetation Management (Regrowth Clearing Moratorium) Act 2009*, (Qld) s2.

[48] The traditional presumption and fundamental rule of English law *nova constitutio futuris formam imponere debet, non praeteritis* meaning a new law should be prospective not retrospective is expounded in G Granville Sharpe & B Galpin, *Maxwell on The Interpretation of Statutes,* Sweet and Maxwell, London, 1953, (10th ed), pp.213-215. The general legal presumption that parliament is presumed to legislate prospectively is considered in FKH Maher, PL Waller & DP Derham, *Cases and Materials on the Legal Process,* Law Book Co, Australia, 1966, pp. 372 -381. A general coverage of retrospectivity in Australia is provided in: AI MacAdam and TM Smith, *Statutes,* Butterworths, Sydney, 1993,(3rd ed,) pp.120 -137 and DC Pearce & RS Geddes, *Statutory Interpretation in Australia,* Butterworths, Sydney, 1996, (4th ed,), chapter 10.

[49] s3 (b) and (g) *Legislative Standards Act 1992* (Qld).

[50] *Parliament of Queensland Act 2001*(Qld) s103.

[51] *Legislative Standards Act 1992(Qld)* s4 (1).

[52] Queensland, Legislative Assembly, Legislation Alert 02/09, pp.85-86, Viewed 4 June 2009 <http://www.parliament.qld.gov.au/view/committees/SLC.asp?SubArea=alerts>.

[53] *Vegetation Management (Regrowth Clearing Moratorium) Bill 2009, Explanatory Notes*, p.2. Viewed on 4 June 2009, <http://www.legislation.qld.gov.au/Bills/53PDF/2009/VegMgtRCMB09Exp.pdf>.

[54] ibid, p.3.

[55] ibid.

[56] Queensland, Legislative Assembly, *Vegetation Management (Regrowth Clearing Moratorium) Bill 2009*. Declared Urgent: Allocation of time order, p156, 23 April 2009. Viewed 4 June 2009, <http://parlinfo.parliament.qld.gov.au/isysquery/09da03ca-b259-499a-bc7c-f5e6a1c3ca32/1/doc/2009_04_23_WEEKLY.pdf#xml=http://parlinfo.parliament.qld.gov.au/isysquery/09da03ca-b259-499a-bc7c-f5e6a1c3ca32/1/hilite/>.

[57] Queensland, Legislative Assembly, *Vegetation Management (Regrowth Clearing Moratorium) Bill 2009*, per J Spence, p.157, 23 April 2009. Viewed 4 June 2009, <http://parlinfo.parliament.qld.gov.au/isysquery/09da03ca-b259-499a-bc7c-f5e6a1c3ca32/1/doc/2009_04_2WEEKLY.pdf>.

[58] Queensland, Legislative Assembly, *Vegetation Management (Regrowth Clearing Moratorium) Bill 2009*, for example: per J Seeney J, p.175, and per L Cunningham, p.233, 23 April 2009. Viewed 4 June 2009, <http://parlinfo.parliament.qld.gov.au/isysquery/09da03ca-b259-499a-bc7c-f5e6a1c3ca32/1/doc/2009_04_23_WEEKLY.pdf#xml=http://parlinfo.parliam ent.qld.gov.au/isysquery/09da03ca-b259-499a-bc7c-f5e6a1c3ca32/1/hilite/>.

[59] J Kehoe, op.cit. p.392.

[60] M Phelps, 'Regrowth Mapping Flawed', *Queensland Country Life*, 7 May 2009, p.9.

[61] *Vegetation Management (Regrowth Clearing Moratorium) Act*, 2009 s7 provides for the six-month moratorium period and s28 the removal of rights of appeal.

[62] Queensland, Legislative Assembly, Address-in Reply per Hobbs, p.1862-1863, 20 August 2009, viewed 7 October2009, <http://parlinfo. parliament.qld.gov.au/isysquery/fce1a8a2-f984-4163-827b-202165e30859/1 120/list/>.

[63] ibid, p.1862.

[64] Queensland, Legislative Assembly, *Vegetation Management (Regrowth Clearing Moratorium) Bill 2009*, per L Cunningham,. p. 237, 23 April 2009.

[65] Queensland, Legislative Assembly, Address-in Reply per Hobbs, p.1863.

[66] Hobbs, p1863.

[67] *Legislative Standards Act* 1992 (Qld) s 4 (3) (i).

[68] *Vegetation Management (Regrowth Clearing Moratorium) Bill* 2009, Explanatory Notes, p.8.

[69] ibid, p.8.

[70] Australian Bureau of Statistics, viewed 4 June 2009, <http://www.abs.gov. au/Ausstats/abs@.nsf/46d1bc47ac9d0c7bca256c470025ff87/F7635B38F792 374BCA256DEA000539DA?opendocument>.

[71] See, for example, the national land use map in Australian Natural Resource Atlas, viewed 4 June 2009, <http://audit.deh.gov.au/anra/agriculture/ gifs/ag_report/section_1/figure1_2.gif>.

[72] Queensland Government, Department of Employment, Economic Development and Innovation: Forecasting, Analysis and Trends, Prospects update, June2009.

[73] Auspoll research report prepared for the World Wildlife Fund, op.cit. The survey of 1016 participants was conducted in February 2009 and included metropolitan and regional/rural residents.

[74] ibid, p.6.

[75] The environmental significance of the end of broadscale clearing in Queensland is dealt with in: C McGrath, 'Editorial commentary: End of

broadscale clearing in Queensland' *Environmental Planning Law Journal*, vol.24, 2007, pp. 5-13.

[76] Queensland Government, Department of Mines and Energy, Annual Report 2007–08 in particular pp 17-20 and the Queensland Government Mining Journal: Queensland's Resources Explosion (2008) which notes that resource exploration investment has doubled in the past three years from $270 million in 2004-2005 to $563.3 million, Viewed 4 June 2009, <http://www.dme.qld.gov.au/mines/qgmj_spring_2008.cfm>.

[77] G Fuller, 'Coal vs. cropping fight widens' *The Land* (15 October 2008), viewed 4 June 2009, <http://theland.farmonline.com.au/news/national rural/agribusiness-and-general/general/coal-vs-cropping-fight-widens/133318 3.aspx>.

[78] Clearing for mining, or an 'extractive industry' is exempt under the regulatory provisions of both the VMA and the *Integrated Planning Act 1997* (Qld), under the *Environmental Protection Act 1994* (Qld) the conservation status of regional ecosystems may be taken into account if applicable.

[79] J Kehoe, 'Voluntary Agreements in Queensland Australia: Contributing Factors and Current Incentive Schemes', S. Wilkes (ed), *Seeking Environmental Justice*, Rodopi, Amsterdam/New York, 2008.

[80] *Nature Conservation Act* 1992 (Qld) ss 4 & 6.

[81] Bimblebox Nature Refuge, Viewed 4 June 2009, <http://www.bimblebox.org>.

[82] *Nature Conservation (Declaration of Nature Refuges) Regulation 1994,* Part 88, Bimblebox Nature Refuge, Viewed 4 June 2009. <http://www.legislation.qld.gov.au/LEGISLTN/SUPERSED/N/NatureConPd AR94_08A_030509.pdf>.

[83] Ibid, Part 31, Avocet Nature Refuge.

Bibliography

Australian Conservation Foundation, 'Land Clearing in Queensland: The Problem and the Solution'. (Undated).

Bates, G., *Environmental Law in Australia*. Butterworths, Sydney, 2006 (6th ed).

Cogger, H., et al, 'Impacts of Land Clearing on Australian Wildlife in Queensland'. World Wildlife Fund, Australia, 2003.

Electoral and Administrative Review Commission, *Report on Queensland Legislative Assembly Electoral System. Volume 1- The Report.* November 1990.

Evans, R., *A History of Queensland.* Cambridge University Press, Cambridge, 2007.

Fitzgerald, G. E., *Report of a Commission of Inquiry Pursuant to Orders in Council.* Queensland Government Printer, Brisbane, 1989.

———, The Tony Fitzgerald Lecture. 28 July 2009.

Fitzgerald, R., Megarrity, L. & Symons, D., *Made in Queensland, A New History.* University of Queensland Press, 2009.

Granville-Sharpe, G. & Galpin, B., *Maxwell on The Interpretation of Statutes.* Sweet and Maxwell, London, 1953 (10th ed).

Gunningham, N. & Grabosky, P., (eds), *Smart Regulation: Designing Environmental Policy.* Clarendon Press, Oxford, 1998.

Hutton, D., 'The Greens and Electoral Politics'. *Arena Magazine.* (Fitzroy, Vic), No. 22, Apr/ May 1996, pp. 14-16.

Kehoe, J., 'Environmental Law-Making in Queensland: The Vegetation Management Act 1999'. *Environmental and Planning Law Journal.* Vol. 26, 2009, pp. 392-410.

———, 'Voluntary Agreements in Queensland Australia: Contributing Factors and Current Incentive Schemes'. *Seeking Environmental Justice.* Rodopi Press, Amsterdam/ New York, 2008.

Krockenberger, A.K., Kitching, R.L. & Turton, S.M., 'Environmental Crisis: Climate Change and Terrestrial Biodiversity in Queensland'. Cooperative Research Centre for Tropical Rainforest Ecology and Management, Rainforest CRC, Cairns, 2003.

MacAdam, A.I. & Smith, T.M., *Statutes.* 3rd ed., Butterworths, Sydney, 1993.

McGrath, C., 'Editorial Commentary: End of Broadscale Clearing in Queensland'. *Environmental Planning Law Journal.* Vol. 24, 2007, pp. 5-13.

Maher, F.K.H., Waller, P.L. & Derham, D.P., *Cases and Materials on the Legal Process*. Law Book Co, Australia, 1966.

Murphy, D., Joyce, R. & Cribb, M. (eds), *The Premiers of Queensland*. University of Queensland Press, Queensland, 1990.

Pearce, D.C. & Geddes, R.S., *Statutory Interpretation in Australia*. 4th ed, Butterworths, Sydney, 1996.

Stockwell, S., 'The Impact of Optional Preferential Vvoting on the 2001 Queensland State Election'. *Queensland Review.*Vol.10, no.1, May 2003, p. 155.

The Australia Institute, 'Land-Use Change and Australia's Kyoto Target'. Submission to Senate Environment References Committee Inquiry into Australia's Response to Global Warming, 1999.

Techera, E., (ed) *Environmental Law, Ethics and Governance*. Inter-Disciplinary Press, Oxford, 2010.

Wanna, J., 'Democratic and Electoral Shifts in Queensland: Back to First Past the Post Voting'. Governance and Public Policy Research Centre, Griffith University, Brisbane, 2004.

Williams P.D., 'The Greening of the Queensland Electorate?'. *Australian Journal of Political Science*. Vol. 41, no.3, Sept 2006, pp. 325-337.

Wolfe, P.M., Murphy, D.G. & Wright, R.G., *Report of a Review of Land Policy and Administration in Queensland*. Land Policy and Administration Review Committee. Queensland, 1990.

Jo Kehoe is a law lecturer at the Central Queensland University. This paper is part of a doctoral thesis currently being undertaken at the Australian Centre for Environmental Law, Australian National University College of Law. Contact: j.kehoe@cqu.edu.au.

Climate Change Construction & Environmental Accountability

Francine Baker

Abstract
This chapter broadly considers climate change law in the United Kingdom (UK). In particular, the chapter explores the likely effect of the UK *Climate Change Act 2008,* which became law on 1 December 2008, on the property/construction industry, and some issues of environmental justice accountability raised by this legislation. This chapter considers some of the features of this legislation including the object of the Act which is designed to reduce greenhouse gas emissions. By 'greenhouse gas emissions' it refers to the three main sources in the UK, which are electricity generation, transport and heat generation.[1] This chapter then examines aspects of the impact of climate change and the Act on the property/construction industry.[2] This Act purports to set up an independent committee to assess and address climate change issues. This chapter queries the extent of that independence, and suggests that what is needed is an independent climate change watchdog. Although, as this chapter discusses, some corporations may be aware that it pays to make climate change commitments, the property/construction industry faces many challenges, not least the development of an environmental ethic in the industry.

Key Words: Climate Change Act, greenhouse gas emissions, adaptation, energy, construction, property, independent committee, environmental, Kant.

*****

1.   Introduction: Environmental Justice Considerations

The carrying out of a human being's duty to himself or herself and to other human beings cannot be achieved other than through living in harmony with his or her whole environment; which includes the natural environment.[3] To ignore this is to be divorced from what sustains us - a contradiction in terms. It is to sever the quality of being human. In all that we do, we ought to endeavour to protect our environment from the vices of human nature. This is especially needed in industry where the most invasive attacks on our environment are taking place. An environmental ethic needs to be a part of us, to be inculcated from birth by parents, carers, and as part of the education system,[4] if it is to have an impact on what we do; but where do we start to ensure this happens and what are the drawbacks?

Bridget Lewis discusses in this volume the benefits to society of the linkage of human rights with the environment and its governance.[5] Brad

Jessup points out that, judges, legislatures and executives seem more persuaded by factors other than those of an environmental ethic.[6] This chapter is concerned with the impact of climate change law on the construction industry and the accountability of all parties involved, and illustrates this with discussion of the administration of the recent United Kingdom (UK) Climate Change Act 2008.

There is no definition of climate change law, but, importantly, it overlaps with many areas of law. This chapter explains that although climate change regulation may be viewed as a legislative example of environmental ethics in practice, its strict enforcement depends on the governance of individuals by such an ethic, without compromise. It may be that no matter what any global approach manages to achieve, the climate will change considerably over the next 50 years. While the changes seem difficult to predict with any certainty,[7] it would appear that new and existing buildings will have to address a new range of environmental conditions and sea level changes. Nearly half of the main greenhouse gas emissions, in particular carbon dioxide emissions, in the UK, are related to buildings: 27% come from housing, and 73% of which concern space and water heating.[8] Statistics show that approximately 10-13% of greenhouse gas emissions come from the manufacture and transport of construction materials and the construction process.[9] Therefore, it is worthwhile to consider what impact UK measures will have on reducing the carbon footprint of the construction industry in the UK and the impact this has on development of an environmental ethic in practice.

2.   Energy Regulation

Energy production and renewal plays a central role in the UK plan to reduce greenhouse gas emissions. To this end the government created the Department for Energy and Climate Change in October 2008 to take responsibility for all aspects of UK energy policy and global climate change on the UK's behalf.[10] The government is particularly interested in the development of renewable forms of electricity generation. This mainly concerns wind, hydro-electric, wave and solar, but also the use of biomass, which is plant and animal matter, and biogas, which is the gas derived from such plant and animal matter. The *Energy Act 2008*[11] has also been created to administer a range of climate measures concerning renewable heat generation and sustainable electricity generation in order to meet the UK's climate change targets.

UK companies are increasingly looking at the economics of renewable energy. Major corporations are seeking to developing their own sources of renewable electricity generation, or (alternatively) contracting to acquire the output from a renewable generating facility that carries their brand, with onshore wind as the popular choice.[12] Renewable energy projects can be located onsite or nearby offsite. If it is onsite, then electricity is supplied directly to the company. Where it is located offsite, the renewable electricity can be offset against that generated by other company projects. Companies have a varying degree of control over a development and hence there are varying degrees of risk involved. They may only be responsible for the building and running of the project, or they may simply lease land to a third-party developer. But it is vital for the parties involved to consider the contractual arrangements carefully in order to assess the risks and economic viability of renewable energy. The government has supplied an incentive for UK companies to use renewable forms of energy: those who generate renewable electricity will receive Renewables Obligation Certificates, which they can then sell.

A Renewables Obligation Certificate (ROC) is a green certificate issued to an accredited generator for eligible renewable electricity generated within the United Kingdom and supplied to customers within the United Kingdom by a licensed electricity supplier. One ROC is issued for each megawatt hour (MWh) of eligible renewable output generated.[13]

Property developers may also be increasingly required to explain how they will source renewable energy. They may need to and it is environmentally ethical to provide for the inclusion of forms of low carbon distributed energy in their tenders for new developments. This should be a requirement of a successful tender. It is usual for local council policies to require that 10% of the energy required for a new building (both residential and non-residential development) be obtained from renewable resources.[14] The *Planning and Energy Act 2008,* which came into force on the 13 November 2008 endorses the legality of such policies.[15] The Act gives local councils in England and Wales powers to set reasonable energy-efficiency standards which developments in their area must comply with, and which are permitted to be greater than the energy requirements of building regulations. The Act also permits local Councils to require that part of the energy used in a development project is renewable energy, and that part is sourced from low-carbon energy sources in the locality. The Council policies should be flexible enough to allow for renewable energy and low-carbon requirements to be supplied from either the locality or the immediate development site. It is also increasingly common in the UK for a developer to commission a third party or to incorporate a company to finance, build and operate an energy services scheme to provide heat and electricity exclusively to the development's tenants. A variety of different community-owned or public-private partnership delivery structures have been developed. These include wind farms established to generate income for communities and Combined Heat and Power (CHP) to deliver cheaper, low carbon energy. Other structures usually install, finance and manage community energy systems to deliver improved efficiency and cheaper fuel. They are generically termed Energy

Service Companies (ESCOs). The London Energy Partnership provides information on successful schemes, but no standard organisational structure for ESCOs has been developed in the UK. Natural gas or biomass fired combined heat and power stations are popular sources of sustainable electricity generation options. A developer may also commission a third party (or incorporate its own subsidiary) to act as an energy services company. The ESCO then finances, builds and operates the scheme - supplying the heat and electricity to the development's tenants on an exclusive basis.[16]

Since 4 January 2009, an Energy Performance Certificate (EPC) is required for construction of all new homes. The certificate is considered important because even minor changes in energy performance when added up will significantly reduce energy consumption and help sustain our environment. However, it is particularly important with the use of buildings as the way the use of lighting heating and the duration of use contribute to nearly half of the UK's energy consumption.[17] An EPC is also required when buying or selling a home or renting, if it is being let for the first time after 1 October 2008. The EPC should state how energy efficient the building is and be accompanied by a recommendation report and a rating that provides a number of measures such as low and zero carbon generating systems that can be undertaken to improve the energy rating. A rating is also given which states the rating that could be achieved the advised measures are implemented.

The certificate is important because nearly 50 per cent of the UK's energy consumption and carbon emissions arise from the way our buildings are lit, heated and used. Even comparatively minor changes in energy performance and the way we use each building will have a significant effect in reducing energy consumption.[18]

Emissions trading schemes are being used to reduce greenhouse gas emissions. The UK Emissions Trading Scheme was launched by Department for the Environment, Food and Rural affairs (Defra) in April 2002 and the EU Emissions Trading Scheme began on 1 January 2005.[19] The rationale is to ensure that the emission reductions take place where the cost of the reduction is low. Emission trading allows the Government to set the overall cap for the scheme, and to give companies the flexibility to trade allowances, so that overall emissions reductions are achieved in a cost-effective way. It imposes emission limit values on particular facilities, and gives companies the flexibility to devise strategies to meet emission reduction targets; for example, by reducing emissions on site, or by buying allowances from other companies who have excess allowances. Companies that participate in the scheme may be allocated an allowance representing a tonne of the relevant emission, for example, carbon dioxide equivalent. They are allowed to exceed their allocation of allowances by purchasing allowances from the market but if it emits less than its allocation of allowances, the surplus allowances can be sold. This arrangement does not impact on the environmental outcome, because the amount of allocated allowances is fixed.[20]

In addition, in October 2008, the British Standards Institution (BSI) published a publicly available specification 'PAS 2050'.[21] This document specifies requirements for the assessment of the carbon footprint of goods and services, i.e., the life cycle GHG emissions of products. It is also supported by Defra and the Carbon Trust.[22] A carbon footprint concerns the greenhouse gas emissions produced or connected with a product or business. Companies will need to consider their rights in relation to their suppliers to require reductions in emissions and to audit compliance with the document. The analysis of a carbon footprint of a product will also require an assessment of the emissions associated with each stage of its production and supply. However, as a reduction of greenhouse gas emissions of a business or product cannot always be achieved, offsetting can play a part in greenhouse gas emission management. Offsetting is achieved by acquiring and cancelling (or retiring) Certified Emissions Reduction certificates, so that no-one else can rely on them to make further offsetting claims. Offsetting schemes fund projects that are either preventative, to stop the release of emissions, e.g., by planting trees that will absorb carbon dioxide or by developing a wind farm instead of using fossil fuel, or by attempting to remove emissions. Many successful schemes use credits recognised by Defra's draft *Code of Best Practice for Carbon Offsetting*, such as the Certified Emissions Reduction certificates, and European Union Allowances and Emission Reduction Units.[23]

3.   The Climate Change Act

The *Climate Change Act 2008* is mainly aimed at giving guidance to public sector organisations about the management of and the adaption to the impact of climate change in the UK, but such guidance will also be useful for the private sector. The Act sets legally binding targets to reduce the UK's greenhouse gas emissions. They concern five year 'carbon budgets', which are supposed to gradually limit the total greenhouse gas emissions. However, the Act does not ensure total reduction. It is only concerned with a certain degree of carbon reduction by 2050. By referring to a 'duty' below, the Act is saying that the government has a legal duty to assess the risks of climate change to the UK and to ensure their reduction.

PART 1: Carbon Target and Budgeting

(1) It is the duty of the Secretary of State to ensure that the net UK carbon account for the year 2050 is at least 80% lower than the 1990 baseline.

(2) The 1990 baseline' means the aggregate amount of -

(a) net UK emissions of carbon dioxide for that year, and

(b) net UK emissions of each of the other targeted greenhouse gases for the year that is the base year for that gas.[24]

The UK government proposes to achieve targets through a number of measures involving an increased use of renewable energy and carbon pricing, some of which have been discussed above. One prominent view is that the measures implemented under the Act are insufficiently pro-active. Critics believe its provisions will not achieve climate change quickly enough, that the targets are too low, and that we should not wait even another five years.[25] 2020 is a long time away. Action is arguably urgently required now.

So, why is there procrastination? It may have to do with governments' emphasis on maintaining a smooth thriving capitalist world economy. Markets are being given the time to adjust to the impact of climate change legislative requirements or to find ways of making green money. This is time we can ill afford to squander, if we are to definitely preserve this planet for future generations. Yet some consider addressing climate change issues as only one of a number of competing issues.

However, climate change is a long-term problem and the current momentum will have to be maintained for years. This will be difficult. Inevitably, other issues will come to the fore, competing for resources and ministerial attention. We already see some of these dynamics at work in efforts to deal with the present economic crisis, although encouragingly climate change has remained on the political agenda. In fact, a powerful case has been made for low-carbon investments as an effective way to kick-start the flagging world economy (Bowen et al 2009, Edenhofer and Stern 2009).[26]

Yet, surely, addressing climate change should be given top priority. Enough has already been written about the cost of and the miniscule impact of low-carbon investments on addressing climate change.[27] It has been argued that it is generally easier to obtain international agreement for a globally-linked trading scheme than for a global carbon tax.[28] However, the price for carbon has been low recently, and in an uncertain market, trading schemes, such as the European Emissions Trading Scheme, have not promoted much investment in low carbon technology. It has yet to be seen whether other initiatives such as a combined system of taxes, to ensure a minimum carbon price and trading, will limit the overall costs.[29] However, a hybrid carbon tax and trading scheme seems a currently favoured alternative,[30] and leading firm PricewaterhouseCoopers LLP argues that it would provide the certainty of a minimum carbon price as well as a safety valve to limit overall costs.[31]

Under the *Climate Change Act*, the Government must take into account of the advice of a supposedly independent Committee on Climate Change (CCC). This Committee is established under the Act to advise the Government on setting carbon budgets and to report to Parliament on the progress made in reducing greenhouse gas emissions.[32] It has a very broad remit regarding the matters it is to advise on under s.34 in connection with carbon budgets:

s. 34

(1) It is the duty of the Committee to advise the Secretary of State, in relation to each budgetary period, on-
   (a) the level of the carbon budget for the period,
   (b) the extent to which the carbon budget for the period should be met-
      (i) by reducing the amount of net UK emissions of targeted greenhouse gases, or
      (ii) by the use of carbon units that in accordance with regulations under sections 26 and 27 may be credited to the net UK carbon account for the period,
   (c) the respective contributions towards meeting the carbon budget for the period that should be made—
      (i) by the sectors of the economy covered by trading schemes (taken as a whole);
      (ii) by the sectors of the economy not so covered (taken as a whole), and
   (d) the sectors of the economy in which there are particular opportunities for contributions to be made towards meeting the carbon budget for the period through reductions in emissions of targeted greenhouse gases.

(2) In relation to the budgetary period 2008-2012, the Committee must also advise the Secretary of State on-
   (a) whether it would be consistent with its advice on the level of the carbon budget for the period to set a carbon budget such that the annual equivalent for the period was lower than the 1990 baseline by 20%, and
   (b) the costs and benefits of setting such a budget.

(3) Advice given by the Committee under this section must also contain the reasons for that advice.

(4) The Committee must give its advice under this section-
(a) for the budgetary periods 2008-2012, 2013-2017
and 2018-2022, not later than 1st December 2008;

Under s.37 of the Act the Secretary of State must lay before
Parliament a response to the points raised by each report of the Committee
under s. 36 (reports on progress) but before doing so, the Secretary of State
must consult the other national authorities on a draft of the response. It
would, therefore, on the face of it, seem that the Committee has potentially
much power and freedom to implement climate change measures. Under s.39

(1) of the Act it may do anything that appears to it
necessary or appropriate for the purpose of, or in
connection with, the carrying out of its functions. S.39
goes on to explain that the
Committee may-

(2) (a) enter into contracts,
(b) acquire, hold and dispose of property,
(c) borrow money,
(d) accept gifts, and
(e) invest money.

(3) In exercising its functions, the Committee may-
(a) gather information and carry out research an
analysis,
(b) commission others to carry out such activities, and
(c) publish the results of such activities carried out by
the Committee or others.

Under subsection (4) the Committee 'must have regard to the
desirability of involving the public in the exercise of its functions'. To what
extent is not clarified. The Committee consists of a prominent group of
experts in relevant fields well-equipped to deal with climate change issues. It
has recently made a progress report to Parliament, which looks impressive on
paper, and next year's work involves a number of further reports, including a
'UK aviation emissions review', 'Advice to the Scottish Government on
emissions reduction targets', and 'Advice on the second phase Carbon
Reduction Commitment (CRC) cap' as well as the Annual report to
Parliament.[33] Given also, its broad powers under the Act, the Committee
would therefore appear to be a force to be reckoned with. However, under S.
41 of the Act, both national bodies and the Secretary of State can give

guidance and directions to the Committee. The Secretary of State also has the final say about energy-efficient polices - and not the Committee. Therefore, the Committee cannot not have the impact an independent watchdog could possibly make on climate change. It is not a climate change watchdog. The government does not have to act on the Committee's advice. They did not, for example, endorse the CCC's intended target of 42%:

> In spring 2009, the government adopted the CCC's 34% interim target for 2008-2022. It acknowledged that the interim target would have to be revised once there is a new international agreement, but it did not endorse the CCC's intended target of 42%. Instead, the CCC will be asked for an updated recommendation once the details of the new agreement are known.[34]

So despite the apparent wide ranging powers given to an apparently independent committee of supposed experts, the Government can direct what the Committee must take into account in reaching its decisions, and it does not have to follow the Committee's recommendations. It therefore seems that despite the Committee's scrutiny of and assessment of what climate change measures should be implemented, the government has the last word regarding the extent of their implementation, if at all. If the UK Government will have to implement a 42% reduction budget soon anyway, the argument as to why it will not do this, now, is unclear. It is common knowledge that delay risks 'locking-in' bad practices. It would also set a good political example to everyone involved in the post-Kyoto treaty negotiations.

4.   An Independent Watchdog

What is needed in the UK and all countries is a genuinely, independent climate change watchdog. This must be a financially independent body, which would need to be set up through legislation by the government. If set up through donations it could be subject to the vested interests of its benefactors. This would obviously be unsatisfactory and may compromise key climate change measures. It needs to be a body whose decisions are free from government or corporate influence and whose decisions can be implemented without either's approval. Perhaps, this could involve a structure and powers analogous to that given to institutions such as the Australian Competition and Consumer Commission (ACCC). The latter is an independent statutory authority of the Government of Australia. It was established in 1995 with the amalgamation of the Australian Trade Practices Commission (TPC) and the Prices Surveillance Authority to administer the *Trade Practices Act 1974* (Cth). It consists of a chairman, deputy chairs, full-time members, ex officio and associate members. Its primary responsibility is to ensure that individuals and businesses comply with the Commonwealth's competition, fair trading and consumer protection laws.[35] The ACCC recommends dispute resolution, but it has the power to initiate legal action when necessary.[36] Similarly a new climate change watchdog could involve various committees of experts (depending on the area of climate change concern) which would decide on measures to reduce the impacts of and to protect victims of climate change. It would have the power to engage in dispute resolution and if necessary, of its own volition, initiate legal action to protect the environment?

So, why not an independent statutory authority to implement climate change? The government may well argue that enough is being is done already through its Department for Energy and Climate Change, which was formed in October 2008 to devise energy policy and climate change mitigation policy under one roof. It has a number of initiatives. On 28 September 2009 it launched-

> the Low Carbon Communities Challenge, a two-year programme to provide financial and advisory support to 20 'test-bed' communities in England, Wales and Northern Ireland that are seeking to cut carbon emissions.[37]

However, the rebuttal argument remains the same. It may also be that a privately funded authority may be more productive than an independent statutory body. Greenpeace is a successful and flourishing non-governmental organisation, which organises campaigns to prevent climate change, amongst many environmentally friendly goals. It is supported by voluntary donations, which are apparently vetted, as it says 'it does not accept donations which could compromise our independence, aims, objectives or integrity'.[38] This is a global organisation, which makes sense, as climate change is ultimately a global problem, and should therefore be considered not just a localised but a global responsibility. Unlike national governments, it is not hampered by political handicaps that negotiating governments face in implementing an environmentally friendly agenda. It seems to work genuinely independently. However it does not have power that governments can utilise to implement climate change measures.

Under Part 4 of the *Climate Change Act* the government has what is called an adaptation reporting power. What this means is that it can require public sector organisations and statutory undertaking companies, like water and energy utilities, to produce a report on how their organisation is assessing as well as acting on the risks and impacts of climate change to their work. If the government considers that the information provided is inadequate, then it can request further information. The government will publish the reports but not every organisation may be required to report. When an organisation is asked to report, they are therefore likely to have the public's full attention. This is likely to be a further motivation for action. Any organisation which has produced a report will then have a duty to comply with that report in its ongoing operations and so provide another key factor in motivating change. This is an example of where the law may facilitate a change in behaviour and the development of an environmental ethic.

But the Secretary of State decides whether or not a report is required. This decision is apparently to be based on whether the organisation is already reporting on adaptation, and on the level of progress being made on adaptation by that reporting authority. However, what constitutes 'best practice' in an ethical sense can only be judged according to the context in which the practices will be implemented, the level of understanding and education of those implementing them, the resources available and the existence of supporting legislation.[39] There are many vested interests at stake which may influence the Government's decision as to which organisation must report. Given the urgency of the issue of addressing climate change, perhaps the Government should pass this power to an independent body to exercise. An independent watchdog could be established, which can determine which organisations need to report, or be inspected and which has the power to enforce such decisions. It should account for its actions in regular government audits, but its actions could be subject to judicial scrutiny rather than a government right of veto. The Government may still then have the final say in whether or not certain organisations should complete reports or are to be inspected, but Government action would be monitored and checked by the watchdog; and ultimately the voting electorate.

The adaptation power also impacts on the construction industry. As a result of the *Climate Change Act*, the industry could be required to reduce carbon emissions during the construction process and to ensure reduction of carbon emissions over the life of the consideration of the constructed product, be it machinery or buildings. The reliance of the construction industry on transportation of materials is another issue, because the transport sector has the fastest growing emissions.[40] Present Government technical solutions to this problem involve a move from fossil fuel-based combustion engines to electric vehicles, biofuels or hydrogen technology. However this strategy has been undermined because car manufacturers across the EU have adhered to a voluntary agreement to abide reduce new car emissions.[41] The difficulty is that transport has many commercial and private stakeholders.

With regard to developers, it is likely that local authorities will introduce increasingly stringent planning regulations. They should also require construction companies to generate an increasing proportion of energy on site. In the UK we have seen the implementation of the Energy Performance of Building Directive (EPBD) which required energy certificates for all buildings by January 2009. But although industry experts will now face increasing scrutiny from the government and the public to ensure carbon dioxide emission reduction targets are met, a greater problem is how to ensure corporate responsibility, in the form of client responsibility. The Welsh Assembly Government has set an example which property/construction clients will need to heed as it recently used the planning system to set a national standard for sustainability for most new buildings in Wales from the 1 September 2009. Their policy will reduce carbon emissions through energy efficiency, the use of renewable energy, and reductions in the consumption of water and the use of more sustainable materials. This is expected to achieve a reduction by more than 31 per cent compared to current building regulations. Housing proposals will also be expected to meet the *Code for Sustainable Homes* Level 3, and non domestic buildings will be expected to meet the Building Research Establishment Environmental Assessment Method Measures (BREEAM) 'Very Good' standard as a minimum. This measures the environmental impact of a building throughout its life.[42] In addition, more than 50 representatives of the building sector, in the UK's first green building charter, announced November 2008, have committed themselves to progress towards a built environment that contributes low or zero net carbon emissions as practically possible.[43]

The Construction industry generally recognises the need to respond to the market, and is readily adapting to meet the demand for green products and services.[44] Indeed, it needs to respond quickly to comply with increasing regulations and guidelines. But whereas the industry is being increasingly regulated, client responsibility to reduce emissions is less evident. The so-called 'brand development' motivator for attracting customers and staff is still a relatively minor factor in generating client interest in reducing carbon emissions. Rather than see climate change as an opportunity for the use of new innovative green products, the interest of homeowners and building users is still generally lagging.[45] The private sector does not generally manage vulnerability to climate risks or plan ahead for the long term life of the building, nor does it as yet generally locally source construction materials. A requirement to use locally sourced materials wherever possible could be drafted into standard contracts, such the New Engineering Contract (NEC), the Joint Contracts Tribunal (JCT) contracts and the Institute of Engineers contracts (ICE) but the agreement of both parties is required for it t be a binding contractual requirement. All parties involved in a construction project, from manufacturers, engineers, specifiers and developers, the main contractor and sub-contractors should share the responsibility for reducing the carbon emissions generated by the UK's construction industry. Sourcing materials locally will obviously reduce, perhaps even significantly reduce the carbon footprint of projects. An environmental ethic would require that consumers contribute to the implementation of climate change measures by being content with local items. Failing that they may participate in local carbon trade schemes, thereby reducing problems of traceability and accountability associated with the import of goods. But the reality may be that both clients and the construction industry need an incentive to work together in 'managing climate risks', and in preparing for climate change scenarios, if there is to be a significant reduction in carbon emissions. This may be partly resolved by the development of an environmental ethic, similar to codes of ethics devised for banks and financial institutions. It will need to go hand in hand with tight regulation and monitoring through legislation and sanctions enforced by genuinely, government-independent statutory watchdogs.

The *Climate Change Act* requires that public investment in buildings and infrastructure take into account the economic costs of climate change. This indicates that there will be huge associated increases in capital and production costs for construction companies. Consequently, the overall impact of these costs and risk assessments will need to be built into contracts with clients with the likelihood of increased professional indemnity insurance costs to provide incentives to reduce risk. Increased project costs due to compliance with climate change measures may also be partly met by a reduction in energy consumption; however, equity cannot be achieved without the co-operation of vested interests, and a communal interest in the local environment.

5.   Conclusion

In conclusion, the property and construction industry will need to quickly develop long term, resource efficiency methods to address the impact of climate change over the lifetime of the property. Increasing Building Regulation requirements is not enough to achieve this. There is also the need to ensure that there is responsible production and consumption of energy, which will require the co-operation of the public and private sectors. There is also the need for the development of and adherence to an ethic of distributive environmental justice. This would exert pressure on the property and the construction industry and their clients to co-operate in promoting climate change efficiently, economically and accountably.

It is a case of everyone in the industry needing to unite through an environmental ethos to ensure that there is minimal impact on the environment, not just through the selection of energy efficient construction materials, but through changing the whole construction environment and process. The problem however, remains that sound climate change measures can lose out to the influence of powerful vested interests, whereby apparently 'extreme' measures are rejected in favour of long term, but too late, phasing in of energy efficient policies. This is where the wide scope of powers given to the CCC under the *Climate Change Act* could be exercised with innovative results, as long as their recommendations are not subject to government veto or a ministerial watering down. There may be no politically efficient way to implement climate change measures quickly, but an independent body with the power of enforcements may yet make a difference. The existence of climate change regulation does not in itself prove that a society has embraced a proactive environmental ethic. Such an ethic has yet to develop to the extent that it makes an impact at grass roots level and to do so, it will need to be part of the fabric of a global society, at all levels.

Notes

[1] Department of Business, Enterprise and Regulatory Reform, *Renewable energy in 2007,* June 2008, Viewed 5 June 2009, <http://www.berr.gov.uk/files/file46685.pdf>.

[2] Office of Public Sector Information, 'Climate Change Act 2008', *Legislation*, 26 November 2008, Viewed 5 June 2009, <http://www.opsi.gov.uk/acts/acts2008/ukpga_20080027_en_1>.

[3] I Kant, 'The Metaphysics of Morals', *Practical Philosophy*, *The Cambridge Edition to the Works of Immanuel Kant*, Cambridge University Press, 1996, 6: pp. 442-444.

[4] ibid at 6:pp. 477-486.

[5] B Lewis, 'The Role of Human Rights in Environmental Governance: The Challenge of Climate Change', *Environmental Law, Ethics and Governance*, E. Techera (ed.), Inter-Disciplinary Press, Oxford, 2010.

[6] B Jessup, 'Investing the Law with an Environmental Ethic: Using an Environmental Justice Theory for Change', *Environmental Law, Ethics and Governance*, E. Techera (ed.), Inter-Disciplinary Press, Oxford, 2010.

[7] See, for example, the UK Climate Impacts Programme website, 2010, last Viewed on 3 March 2010, <http://www.ukcip.org.uk>.

[8] F Maunsell, Sustainable Development Commission, W Dixon & HBF, *DTI* Viewed 5 March 2010, <http://www.berr.gov.uk/files/file37180.pdf>, pp.1-2.

[9] ibid.

[10] See the Department of Energy and Climate Change website, 2010, viewed 3 March 2010, <http://www.decc.gov.uk/>.

[11] Office of Public Sector Information, 'Energy Act 2008', *Legislation*, 26 November 2008, Viewed 22 July 2009, <www.opsi.gov.uk/acts/acts2008/ukpga_20080032_en_1>.

[12] OilVoice News Item, 'The Schneider Corporation Adds Wind Energy to Services', OilVoice, Monday, July 20, 2009, Viewed 4 March 2010 <http://www.oilvoice.com/n/The_Schneider_Corporation_Adds_Wind_Energy_to_Services/987f8c47.aspx>.

[13] Office of the Gas and Electricity Markets, 'Renewables Obligation', Office of the Gas and Electricity Markets, Viewed 4 March 2010, <http://www.of gem.gov.uk/Sustainability/Environment/RenewablObl/Pages/RenewablObl.a spx>.

[14] S Wells, 'Policy SE2 - The 10% Renewables Requirement', Waverley Borough Council, 06/07/2009 12:21, last Viewed 4 March 2010, <http://www.waverley.gov.uk/site/scripts/documents_info.php?documentID= 272>.

[15] Office of Public Sector Information, 'Planning and Energy Act 2008', *Legislation*, 13 November 2008, last viewed 4 March 2010, <http://www. opsi.gov.uk/acts/acts2008/ukpga_20080021_en_1>.

[16] Commission for Architecture and the Built Environment & Urban Practitioners, 'Creating new patterns of ownership (ESCOs and MUSCOs)', Sustainable Cities, Viewed 4 March 2010, <http://www.sustainablecities.org. uk/energy/portfolio/ownership/>.

[17] Communities and Local Government 'Energy Performance of Buildings', *Planning Building and the Environment*, Communities and Local Government, 1 March 2008, Viewed 4 March 2010, <http://www. communities.gov.uk/planningandbuilding/theenvironment/energyperformanc e/>.

[18] Communities and Local Government, 'Energy Performance Certificates and New Homes: A Builder's Guide', *Planning Building and the Environment*, Communities and Local Government, Viewed 4 March 2010 <http://www.communities.gov.uk/publications/planningandbuilding/epcsbuil dersguide>.

[19] Department for Environment Food and Rural Affairs, 'The Community Emissions Trading Scheme', *Department for Environment Food and Rural Affairs,* 30 July 2008, Viewed 23 July 2009, <http://www.defra. gov.uk/news/2008/080729a.htm>.

[20] ibid.

[21] British Standards Institute, 'PAS 2050 - Assessing the life cycle greenhouse gas emissions of goods and services', British Standards Institute, Viewed 23 July 2009, <http://www.bsigroup.com/Standards-and-Publications/How-we-can-help-you/Professional- AS-2050>.

[22] Carbon Trust, 2009, Viewed 3 March 2010, <http://www. carbontrust.co.uk/Pages/Default.aspx?gclid=CMzaje7NoaACFRlBlAod-FvH aQ>.

[23]Summaries of EU legislation 'Greenhouse gas emission allowance trading scheme', *Summaries of EU Legislation,* Europa, 7 March 2008, Viewed 5 March 2010, <http://europa.eu/legislation_summaries/energy/european_ energy_policy/l28012_en.htm>.

[24] Office of Public Sector Information, 'The Climate Change Act 2008', op.cit.

[25] A Giddens, S Latham & R Liddle (eds), *Building a Low-Carbon Future: The Politics of Climate Change,* Policy Network, London, 2009, Viewed on 8 August 2009, <http://politicsofclimatechange.files.wordpress.com/2009/06/building-a-low-carbon-future-pamphlet-web.pdf> pp. 14-15 and p. 111.

[26] S Frankhauser, D Kennedy & J Skea, 'The UK's Carbon Targets for 2020 and Role of the Committee of Climate Change', *Building a Low-Carbon Future: The Politics of Climate Change,* 2009, Viewed 5 March 2010, <http://politicsofclimatechange.files.wordpress.com/2009/06/building-a-low-carbon-future-pamphlet-web.pdf>, Chapter 10, p. 99.

[27] G Hack, 'The Debate Surrounding Patents and Low-Carbon Technology, *Clean and Sustainable Technologies Group,* 20 April, 2009, Viewed 5 March 2010, <http://cleanip.com.au/2009/04/20/the-debate-surrounding-patents-low-carbon-technology-is-heating-up/>.

[28] T Kunzemann (ed.), 'Trade or Tax? How to Get Rid of Greenhouse Gases', Allianz Knowledge Partnership, February 9, 2007, Viewed 5 March 2010, <http://knowledge.allianz.com/en/globalissues/energy_co2/emission_trading/emission_trade_or_tax.html>.

[29] T Macalister & A Seager, 'Carbon Trading Undermined by Boom and Bust', *The Guardian,* Monday 23 March 2009, Viewed on 8 August 2009, <http://www.guardian.co.uk/environment/2009/mar/23/carbon-emissions>.

[30] Carbon Finance Global News, 'PwC Calls for Carbon Tax and Trading hybrid', 25 March, 2009, *Carbon Finance,* 2010 Fulton Publishing Ltd, Viewed 5 March 2010, <http://www.carbon-financeonline.com/index.cfm?section=global&action=view&id=11948>.

[31] PriceWaterhouseCoopers, 'Carbon Taxes vs Carbon Trading Pros, Cons and the Case for a Hybrid Approach', *PricewaterhouseCoopers,* International Emissions Trading Associations, March 2009, Viewed 5 March 2010, <http://www.ieta.org/ieta/www/pages/getfile.php?docID=3261>.

[32] Committee on Climate Change website, no date given, Viewed 5 March 2010, <http://www.theccc.org.uk/>.

[33] Committee on Climate Change, 'Meeting Carbon Budgets - The Nneed for a Step Change: Progress Report to Parliament on Climate Change: 'Executive Summary', the Committee of Climate Change, 9 October 2009, Viewed 5 March 2010, <http://hmccc.s3.amazonaws.com/docs/21667%20CCC%20Executive%20Summary%20AW%20v4.pdf>.

[34] Frankhauser et al, op.cit. p.109.

[35] Australian Competition and Consumer Commission, 'What we Do: Roles and Activitis', Commonwealth of Australia, 2009, Viewed 10 March 2010, <http://www.accc.gov.au/content/index.phtml/itemId/54137>.

[36] Ibid.

[37] Department of Energy and Climate Change, 'Low Carbon Communities Challenge', Department of Energy and Climate Change, 5 March 2010, 5 March 2010, <http://www.decc.gov.uk/en/content/cms/what_we_do/consumers/lc_communities/lc_communities.aspx>.

[38] Greenpeace UK, 'About Greenpeace', Greenpeace UK, <http://www.greenpeace.org.uk/about>, 8 March 2010, Viewed 10 March 2010, and <http://www.greenpeace.org.uk/about/greenpeace-environmental-trust>.

[39] R Hitchins, 'Defining a Best Practice Approach' in a report for the Royal Institution of Chartered Surveyors by the Building Research Establishment, June 2008, Royal Institute of Chartered Surveyors, 2010, Viewed on 10 March 2010, <http://www.rics.org/site/scripts/download_info.aspx?fileID=4128&categoryID=523>.

[40] HM Treasury, 'Annex 7.c Emissions from the transport sector', HM Treasury, Viewed 5 March 2010, <www.hm-treasury.gov.uk/d/Transport_annex.pdf>; Climate-L.org, 'ADB backed Conference backs calls on Transport Sector to Curb Emissions', May 2009, site last updated 2010, Viewed 5 March 2010, <http://climate-l.org/2009/06/02/adb-backed-conference-calls-on-transport-sector-to-curb-emissions/>.

[41] Frankhauser et al., op.cit., p. 107.

[42] S Roy, Centre for Construction Innovation, *BREEAM Assessing the Environmental Performance of Buildings,* p.2, last Viewed 28 February 2010, <http://www.ccinw.com/images/publications/Intro_BREEAM.pdf>.

[43] Welsh Assembly Government, 'Wales first in UK to set national green standards', Viewed 5 March 2010, <http://www.wales.com/en/content/cms/News/Wales_first_in_UK/Wales_first_in_UK.aspx>.

[44] Institute of Civil Engineers, 'Why Waste Heat', Institute of Civil Engineers, May 2009, Viewed 5 March 2010, <http://www.ice.org.uk/downloads/heat_report.pdf> at p. 3- 'Based on our research report ICE makes five recommendations to government and industry to improve efficiency in the heat sector: Government should commission a feasibility study into capturing heat and creating a district heating network at Drax, Ferrybridge and Eggborough, and Tilbury-Kingsnorth. The assessment of heat capture potential should become a planning condition on all new power stations. Local authorities should map current and future heat demand in their area. Government should conduct a review to establish if CO2 and renewable targets are pulling in opposite directions. Government should encourage the use of lower carbon intensity fuel sources for heating domestic and commercial property'.

[45] There are of course noteworthy exceptions. For example, R, Smithers states that 'M&S''s 'Plan A', a five-year, 'eco plan' under which, by 2012, M&S aims to become carbon neutral; send no waste to landfill; extend sustainable sourcing and set new standards in ethical trading' in 'Marks & Spencer Launches UK's Greenest till Roll New M&S Receipts are Lighter and Use 8% Less Pulp – Helping to Save more than 800 Trees a Year', *The Guardian*, Wednesday 15 April 2009, Viewed on 6 June 2009, <http://www.guardian.co.uk/environment/2009/apr/15/marks-and-spencer-sustainble-till-rolls>.

Bibliography

Australian Competition and Consumer Commission, 'What we Do: Roles and Activities'. *Commonwealth of Australia.* 2009, Viewed 10 March 2010, <http://www.accc.gov.au/content/index.phtml/itemId/54137>.

British Standards Institute, 'PAS 2050 - Assessing the Life Cycle Greenhouse Gas Emissions of Goods and Services'. Viewed 23 July 2009 <http://www.bsigroup.com/Standards-and-Publications/How-we-can-help-you/Professiona l -Standards-Service/PAS-2050>.

Carbon Finance Global News, 'PwC Calls for Carbon Tax and Trading Hybrid'. *Carbon Finance.* 2010 Fulton Publishing Ltd, 25 March, 2009, Viewed 5 March 2010, <http://www.carbon-financeonline.com/index.cfm?section=global&action=view&id=11948>.

Commission for Architecture and the Built Environment & Urban Practitioners, 'Creating New Patterns of Ownership (ESCOs and MUSCOs)'. Sustainable Cities. Viewed 4 March 2010, <http://www.sustainablecities.org.uk/energy/portfolio/ownership/>.

Committee on Climate Change, 'Meeting Carbon Budgets – The Need for a Step Change: Progress Report to Parliament on Climate Change: Executive Summary'. 9 October 2009, Viewed 5 March 2010, <http://hmccc.s3.amazonaws.com/docs/21667%20CCC%20Executive%20Summary%20AW %20v4.pdf>.

Communities and Local Government, 'Energy Performance of Buildings'. *Planning Building and the Environment.* Communities and Local Government, 1 March 2008, Viewed 4 March 2010, <http://www.communities.gov.uk/planningandbuilding/theenvironment/energyperformance/>.

——, 'Energy Performance Certificates and New Homes: A Builder's Guide'. *Planning Building and the Environment.* Communities and Local Government, Viewed 4 March 2010 <http://www.communities.gov.uk/publications/planningandbuilding/epcsbuildersguide>.

Department of Business, Enterprise and Regulatory Reform, *Renewable Energy in 2007.* June 2008, Viewed 5 June 2009, <www.berr.gov.uk/files/file 46685.pdf>.

Department of Energy and Climate Change, 'Low Carbon Communities Challenge'. *Department of Energy and Climate Change.* Viewed on 6 March 2010, <http://www.decc.gov.uk/en/content/cms/what_we_do/consumers/lc_communities/lc_communities.aspx>.

Department for Environment Food and Rural Affairs, 'The Community Emissions Trading Scheme'. 30 July 2008, Viewed on 23 July 2009, <http://www.defra.gov.uk/news/2008/080729a.htm>.

Frankhauser, S., Kennedy, D. & Skea, J., 'The UK's Carbon Targets for 2020 and Role of the Committee of Climate Change'. *Building a Low-Carbon Future: The Politics of Climate Change.* Policy Network, London, 2009, Viewed on 5 March 2010, <http://politicsofclimatechange.files.wordpress.com/2009/06/building-a-low-carbon-future-pamphlet-web.pdf>.

Giddens, A., Latham S. & Liddle R. (eds), *Building a Low Carbon Future: The Politics of Climate Change.* Policy Network, London, 2009, Viewed on 8 August 2009, <http://politicsofclimatechange.wordpress.com/2009/06/15/building-a-low-carbon-future/>.

Hack, G., 'The Debate Surrounding Patents and Low-Carbon Technology. *Clean and Sustainable Technologies Group.* 20 April, 2009, Viewed 5 March 2010, <http://cleanip.com.au/2009/04/20/the-debate-surrounding-patents-and-low-carbon-technology-is-heating-up/>.

Hitchins, R., 'Defining a Best-Practice Approach'. *A Report for the Royal Institution of Chartered Surveyors by the Building Research Establishment.* June 2008, Royal Institute of Chartered Surveyors, 2010, Viewed on 10 March 2010, <http://www.rics.org/site/scripts/download_info.aspx?file ID=4 128&categoryID=523>.

HM Treasury, 'Annex 7.c Emissions from the Transport Sector'. Viewed 10 March 2010, <http://www.hm-treasury.gov.uk/d/Transport_annex.pdf>, <http://www.hm-treasury.gov.uk/d/Transport_annex.pdf>.

Institute of Civil Engineers, 'Why Waste Heat'. Institute of Civil Engineers. May 2009, Viewed 5 March 2010, <http://www.ice.org.uk/downloads/heat_report.pdf>.

Jessup, B., 'Investing the Law with an Environmental Ethic: Using an Environmental Justice Theory for Change'. *Environmental Law, Ethics and Governance*. Techera, E. (ed.), Inter-Disciplinary Press, Oxford, 2010.

Kant, I., 'The Metaphysics of Morals'. *Practical Philosophy*. Gregor, M.J. (trans. & ed.), The Cambridge Edition to the Works of Immanuel Kant, Cambridge University Press, 1996.

Kunzemann T., (ed.)'Trade or Tax? How to Get Rid of Greenhouse Gases'. Allianz Knowledge Partnership. February 9, 2007, Viewed 5 <March 2010, http://knowledge.allianz.com/en/globalissues/energy_co2/emission_trading/emission_trade_or_tax.html>.

Lewis, B., 'The Role of Human Rights in Environmental Governance: The Challenge of Climate Change'. *Environmental Law, Ethics and Governance*. Techera, E. (ed.), Inter-Disciplinary Press, Oxford, 2010.

Macalister T. & Seager A., 'Carbon Trading Undermined by Boom and Bust'. *The Guardian*. Monday 23 March 2009, Viewed on 8 August 2009, <http://www.guardian.co.uk/environment/2009/mar/23/carbon-emissions-ts>.

Office of Public Sector Information, 'Climate Change Act 2008'. *Legislation*. 26 November 2008, Viewed 5 June 2009, <www.opsi.gov.uk/acts/acts2008/ukpga_20080027_en_1>.

Office of Public Sector Information, 'Energy Act 2008'. *Legislation*. 26 November 2008, Viewed 22 July 2009, <www.opsi.gov.uk/acts/acts2008/ukpga_20080032_en_1>.

Office of the Gas and Electricity Markets, 'Renewables Obligation'. Office of the Gas and Electricity Markets. Viewed 4 March 2010 <http://www.ofgem.gov.uk/Sustainability/Environment/RenewablObl/Pages/RenewablObl.aspx>.

Office of Public Sector Information, 'Planning and Energy Act 2008'. *Legislation*. 13 November 2008, Viewed 4 March 2010 <http://www.opsi. gov.uk/acts/acts2008/ukpga_20080021_en_1>.

OilVoice News Item, 'The Schneider Corporation Adds Wind Energy to Services'. *Oil Voice*. Monday, July 20, 2009, Viewed 4 March 2010 <www.oilvoice.com/n/The_Schneider_Corporation_Adds_Wind_Energy_to_ Services/987f8c47.aspx>.

PricewaterhouseCoopers, 'Carbon Taxes vs. Carbon Trading Pros, Cons and the Case for a Hybrid Approach'. *PricewaterhouseCoopers*. International Emissions Trading Associations. March 2009, Viewed 5 March 2010, <http://www.ieta.org/ieta/www/pages/getfile.php?docID=3261>.

Smithers, R., 'Marks & Spencer Launches UK's Greenest Till Roll: New M&S Receipts are Lighter and Use 8% Less Pulp – Helping to Save more than 800 Trees a Year'. *The Guardian*. Wednesday 15 April 2009, Viewed 6 June 2009, <www.guardian.co.uk/environment/2009/apr/15/marks-and-spen cer-sustainble-till-rolls>.

Summaries of EU Legislation 'Greenhouse Gas Emission Allowance Trading Scheme'. *Europa*. 7 March 2008, Viewed 5 March 2010, <http://europa.eu/ legislation_ summaries/energy/european_energy_policy/l28012_en.htm>.

Wells, S., 'Policy SE2 - The 10% Renewables Requirement'. Waverley Borough Council. 06/07/2009 12:21. Viewed 4 March 2010, <http://www. waverley.gov.uk/site/scripts/documents_info.php?documentID=272>.

Welsh Assembly Government, 'Wales First in UK to Set National Green Standards'. Viewed 5 March 2010, <http://www.wales.com/en/content/cms/ News/ Wales_ first_in_UK/Wales_first_in_UK.aspx>.

Francine Baker is a Solicitor, a senior lecturer at London South Bank University and is affiliated with Wolfson College, Oxford.